In Pursuit of

In Pursuit of a Better Life

A New Englander on the Western Frontier

Liz Peretz

Vinca Publishing

First published 2021 by
Vinca Publishing
60 Great Clarendon St
Oxford
OX2 6AX
UK

Paperback
ISBN-13 978-1-8383520-0-4

Printed by Lightning Source LLC
Typesetting by www.preparetopublish.com

Contents

Figure 1: Judah Colt, about 1820.
Source: Sanford, L.G., The History of Erie County (1894).

Illustrations

Acknowledgements

This book was made possible by the generosity of my American cousin, Herbert Spencer, who allowed me to take the yellowing transcripts of Colt's *Journal* and *Narrative* back to the UK with me.

The book has been a long time in the writing. Beth Simmons, a well-established historian of Erie County, and like me a descendant of early settlers, has supported me, and fed me material during all that time – taking me to sources I would have struggled to find, and cheering me on.

Many others have helped, listened to my enthusiasms, made good suggestions, and of these I single out my editor and partner, Bill MacKeith, whose faith in me and the project have made the book possible.

Principal sources

In the 1930s a typewritten transcript of the leather-bound originals Judah Colt's *Journal* and *Narrative* was made under the direction of Judah Colt Spencer of the First National Bank of Erie (my Great Uncle 'J', not the JCS whom Judah Colt made his business heir); at that time the originals were kept in the bank vaults. The whereabouts of the original volumes is not known. Several versions of the typescript exist. For this reason, page numbers are not given.

The *Journal*

Judah Colt (1761–1832) wrote a journal from 1796. It has survived in almost daily detail until 1808, though after this it peters out somewhat and stops altogether in 1811. The *Journal* was written in the knowledge that his employers might ask to see it; it is important to bear that in mind when reading the entries. In the present volume, quotations that include a date are from the *Journal*.

Narrative

Colt wrote his autobiography, probably in 1808 at the age of 47, and called it his 'Narrative'. It was quite common at that time for people on the frontier to write up their backstory for people to read; for family members, fellow settlers, or people back where they came from. The *Narrative* contains some precise dates prior to those covered by the surviving *Journal*. This indicates that Colt was probably referring to a diary or diaries that no longer survive.

Day Book for 1798-9

'Sundry Accounts D. to Penna. Popult Compy for Amount of Outstanding Debts, Bills, recievable.' I am indebted to Beth Simmons for sharing her transcript of Judah Colt's account book which sheds a fascinating light on daily life in a newly colonized township.

The focus of the present volume is 1789–96, his years in Canandaigua, and 1796–1804, his years in Greenfield as land agent before he moved to Erie.

Chapter 1

My connection with Colt, a word on diaries, and current thinking about the north-west frontier

I've had a clutch of yellowing old copies of Judah Colt's *Journal* and his *Narrative* with me for the last 50 years. The cousin who gave them to me is still alive, in his nineties.

Judah Colt (1761–1832) was my grandmother's grandfather's great uncle. I want to introduce you to him, and through him to a moment in the history of finance, of gambling on futures, of 'progress'. A moment of brutal settler colonialism, white male supremacist style, disguised in the language of the time as a glorious moment of 'second creation' – taming the wilderness, bringing civilisation west of the Alleghenies.

Back in the 1820s, the childless Judah Colt prepared one of his great nephews, called Judah Colt Spencer in his great uncle's honour, to take over his land business. Judah Colt Spencer, my direct ancestor, had been raised in the early nineteenth century in Connecticut, and stated in *his* journal how homesick he was when he arrived in Erie to complete his schooling at the new Erie Academy, living with his great aunt and uncle. (Yes – I was given one of *his* journals, too, carefully transcribed for my great-uncle.) As I pieced the time line together, with the help of an array of second cousins, first cousins once removed, and others, I felt as though each new act of these past generations of my family, each new event I was told about, or read about, attached me to the earth more securely. One of my Erie great uncles, Uncle Spike, had been given as a wedding present a wheel chart of his family and that of Rachel his new wife. The new couple, in bold calligraphy, were in the middle of the chart, and whirling around them were their parents, grandparents, great grandparents, uncles, cousins, aunts, like a vast encircling host, holding them up, giving them, for their wedding day and ever after, their own stage. It was very moving to unfurl the chart, the size of a tablecloth, and see my own forebears in there and imagine just such a chart of my own.

I wanted to know more. So I set out on several visits to look at more papers, in libraries, in people's houses – and above all to visit the places, to visit Erie, to visit Old Lyme, Connecticut and the banks of the Connecticut River which Judah Colt and his great nephew knew in their boyhood. And to make the journeys, now taken in the soft comfort of air-conditioned cars on the highways that traverse the Alleghenies, then taken on ancient indigenous American paths, or travelled by boat; and to see the old sites, the eighteenth-century villages, the original houses that were built in the newly marked out land. Over several visits, I found more concrete evidence from the early years. Photographs – taken to mark a family picnic – of Colt's farm in North East – down the road from Greenfield (now Colt's Station) where Colt first established himself in Pennsylvania in 1797. (Sadly, the Greenfield house that Colt describes no longer stands.) The house Colt moved to in Erie in 1804 – relocated to the poorer part of the town down by the lake, in multi-occupation and in need of a lick of paint and some new windows when I saw it in 2012 – has now been reincarnated (see Postscript). The family have now all departed from Erie, but the house where Maud, my own grandmother, spent her early childhood in Erie still exists. It is run as a 'heritage' bed and breakfast, Spencer House. The owners have recreated the house as it was when it was built in the 1860s. I stayed there overnight, in 'the Nanny's Room'.

The more I saw, the more I understood there were more stories – not just the linking of the present sanitised landscape of drive-ins, towns and industrial scrapyards with the mile upon mile of

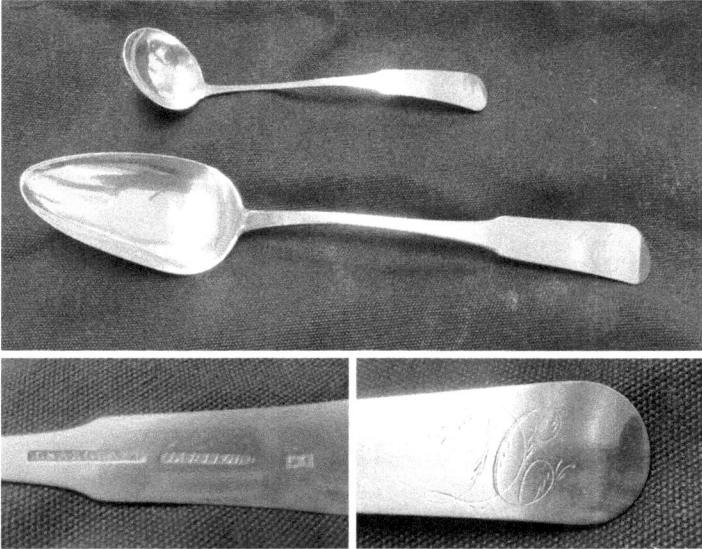

Figures 2–4: Colt family spoons by Jacob Sargeant (1761–1843), silversmith working in Hartford, Conn., 1785/95–1835, with wheatsheaf mark.

rough woodland, marshes and rivers of the eighteenth century, but even earlier than that to the villages of the Americans that were there long before my forebears arrived, with their settled life in clearings by the lake, living 'light touch' on the land, fishing, hunting, growing orchards and crops. And who knows who else was there before, and before them. The big difference brought by Judah Colt and his like was the erection of fences, the assertion of property rights, the 'keep out' signs, the guns – and the recourse to law courts – to keep control. He brought a kind of violence, masquerading as orderliness. His story allows us to see a close-up of this 'rape of the earth' which is with us still, 200 years on, as we watch the Amazon forest ripped up in neat squares, and made over to cattle grazing and crops.

To help my acquaintance with my adopted ancestor, I have some possessions. I have two spoons of the finest, thinnest silver:

a tiny ladle, and a serving spoon, stamped 'Hartford', Conn. Keeping them safe, polished, passed down through the generations. The monogram 'DC' has puzzled me. There are few D. Colts. Colt's sister Deborah (grandmother of Judah Colt Spencer) was one; his mother Desiree Colt, another.

They are now in a glass-fronted cupboard, in England, brought out to marvel at from time to time. I wonder at what meals they would have been produced – with his neighbour 'Sir Timothy Tuttle esquire' (Colt liked to fraternise with people with a handle to their name)? Or were they kept on show, to impress, polished by the 'mulatto' indentured girl? I watch them in my mind at their big dining table in their elegant two-storey clapboard house in Greenfield: two windows on each side of the front door and five on the upper story, all with glass brought by boat from the East Coast (we know this from Colt's company accounts in his Pennsylvania Population Company *Day Book*). We can imagine the guests sitting back on their chairs, with the highly polished solid cherry floor beneath their feet, drinking the port Colt had imported by 'battoe' (flat-bottomed boat) up French Creek from the East, via the Allegheny River. We know from Colt's *Day Book*, which came to light in the late twentieth century, that the house was made by master carpenters Joshua and Sampson Hamilton, assisted by James Henton, 'the main handyman of the settlement'. Not only did they build the house, they also made the cherry wood floors and a dining table; we know from the *Day Book* that Joel Andrews made 20 lights of ash for the kitchen windows in June and another 72 window lights – and settled the glass into the sashes – in October.[1] And then, company departed the following morning, Colt retiring to his office, writing letters to his employers, signed, 'I remain your humble servant Judah Colt Esquire', or to his brothers signed, 'your affectionate Brother, Judah Colt', and ending the office morning with an entry to his diary like this one: 'July 2nd. Lowry

---

[1] Simmons, B. (1997) 'A window opens to Erie's past': "Judah Colt Daybook, Greenfield, 1798-1799"', *Journal of Erie Studies* 26: pp. 5–23.

weather...', before going out on horseback to meet the settlers and see how the Company workmen were doing.

The rest of the household are harder to imagine because Colt mentions them so little. We know that Mrs Colt came from the mouth of the Connecticut River, like Judah; she is described as 'suited to frontier life' in a letter from Judah's brother[2]; we know she had several infant deaths, before her daughter was born. Colt tells us it was her devotion that brought him to religion. We know she travelled to Philadelphia and a few times to Connecticut. And that she had a former slave girl to help her in the house when they moved to Greenfield. We know she had a fall from a sleigh when out with a friend. But she – Mrs Elizabeth Colt, née Marvin – remains a hazy figure. From other sources we know the kind of life she must have led, with all its hardships. The kitchen garden, the dairy, the weaving, sewing bees. We know too from later sources that she was active in running a Sunday school for 'coloured' residents of Erie in the 1820s. We know Colt left her some of his books, so she must have enjoyed reading. We know the boy who came to live with them – Judah Colt Spencer, their Connecticut-born great nephew – loved her dearly – he says so in his journals.

Colt's autobiography, his *Narrative*, suggests to his reader that, while he himself achieved some degree of upward social mobility by moving from Connecticut to Erie, Pennsylvania, his story is one of continuation. The colonial America of his childhood was as much as possible recreated by him and his peers in the frontier settlements, even the architecture and the social hierarchy of labourers and house servants. He also recreated the civil and religious infrastructure of Connecticut. Although he was thrown in with a rougher sort of settler than he had been accustomed to – families from Ireland, ex-soldiers from the US army – he tried to keep most of his social interaction to people of property, whose family had property in the East, who had money and influence. In fact much of the wealth that helped him move up

[2] 7 January 1799, Sanford-Spencer Estate papers, Erie County Historical Society, Hagen Center, Erie.

a social class came from selling 'new' land to old neighbours from the Connecticut seaboard.

To do his words justice – and my own reaction to them, as I share them with you – I need to lay out my own shibboleths, as far as I am conscious of them. While Colt and I are both individual voices, they are both voices of a particular historical time and place, communities – his, late eighteenth-century North America, mine, early twenty-first century Europe , the United Kingdom. His childhood was in colonial Connecticut, where there was increasing irritation with the British rulers. Colt was 15 when independence was finally declared, and 22 when the Treaty of Paris was signed, immediate fighting ceased and the West was opened up. His diaries that survive were mainly written from the age of 27 to the age of 44. As a child in immediate post-World War II austerity Britain, enriched by the new welfare state – free orange juice, cod-liver oil and malt, the taste of my early years – I was awed at the conspicuous consumption of my American relatives. I am writing this in my seventies, at the end of my working life; Colt wrote his *Journal* at the outset of his career. By the time I am writing this, in 2020, 'progress' has become a dirty word to some of us. I believe in an equal society, one which must change radically if we are to face up to the ecological disaster we've created, to embrace a lifestyle in reverse, with private modesty, and only publicly shared luxury. Colt believed in social hierarchy, in making money through hard work, buying and selling land and stock, farming. He believed that sturdy, serious Christian New Englanders were best placed to own and run the frontier communities, with the help of their poorer labourers, artisans, indentured servants and slaves. Europeans who were content to fit in were tolerated; those who challenged the hierarchy were not.

I listen with pain to Colt's excitement about laying out towns and villages in what he describes as the 'wilderness'. How could he not have seen what he was doing? The plunder he was complicit in? How could he have been taken in by the then current views of Native Americans as savages, as children, when the evidence in front of him told a different story? Evidence in the shape of ancient orchards, manifest skills in fishing and crops, and in medicine? How could he have left out, in his writing, servants or slaves or women, who did more than half of the work at the time? And why was he so prejudiced against Europeans – especially the Irish in Pennsylvania? In his writing I see all too clearly the devastation that was occurring on the frontier, the cheating, the use of power – male power – New England Anglo-American power – hidden beneath his words. Words that brim with satisfaction at the neat fields and roads of the new communities – first in 1789 Upper New York State and then, when that land was opened up in the mid 1790s, in Pennsylvania, by Lake Erie.

To understand Judah Colt's words in the *Journal* and *Narrative* a little better, I've turned to Sally Bayley's *The Private Life of the Diary*.[3] She shows, with snippets from diaries across the centuries, that diarists often show us the person they would like to be, rather than the one they are. In the case of Colt, who we know longed to become a 'country gentleman' with all the attendant gravitas, we can deduce that he will show us that face (of key interest for the historian trying to capture the spirit of the age). Bayley also notes that sometimes diaries are written for a particular audience, which explains why some things are left out, others magnified. Throughout the following chapters, I've used Bayley's voice as a guide to the text. What was he trying to hide? Was he writing to show himself and others that he really was a true Anglo American, New England born and bred (with the emphasis on England?) Hiding any event or thought that jarred with this image? Does he ever let the mask slip? Or exaggerate to the point that he stretches his readers' credulity?

---

[3] Bayley, S. (2016) *The Private Life of the Diary: From Pepys to Tweets: A History of the Diary as an Art Form*, London: Random House.

Current thinking about the north-west frontier

There is no way to judge this without some more knowledge of what was happening in the early Republic. The section that follows does poor justice to the wealth of scholarship it attempts to represent, but at least it may provide a rough guide to throw some light on Colt's words.

The 1780s and 90s were extremely problematic for the new Republic. There was victory – of a sort – over the 'mother country'. But there was a gaping hole in the finances at State and Federal level; the 13 states each had their own way of doing things; and to survive, it was necessary to continue international trade, back and forth over the Atlantic, and up and down to the West Indies. To compound the problems, the Revolution – the 'declaration of independence' – had turned the various societies that made up the 13 states topsy-turvy. Some rich landowners had been Loyalists, some Patriots, some had tried to stay out of it. In the New England states, which were highly socially stratified and very 'English' in aspiration, like most imperial colonies, some landowners who were patriots saw their labourers back the British, and vice versa. The Native Americans, to their enormous cost, sided with the British – they probably felt they had been treated better by the 1763 Proclamation Line Law, which protected their rights, than they had been treated by the colonists on the ground.

In the mid-eighteenth century the colonies had become used to conspicuous consumption, egged on by British manufacturers. The British had exported goods from the early years of their industrial revolution to a captive market – their colonies. To keep this going now that the links with Britain were severed would have been very expensive indeed – but there was an opportunity. The states, once the British legal 'yoke' had been lifted, were free to have their own manufacturing boom. But this needed capital – and there was no money. On top of everything else, the New England states in particular were suffering a population explosion of their own. The population was further expanding with a steady flow of hopefuls from hard-pushed Europe – bad harvests, unrest, high taxes, enclosures of land had pushed people over the Atlantic in large numbers.

The pressure on the breakaway colonies was immense. As the wars ended, the country filled with discharged soldiers, who needed to be paid. New infrastructure needed funding. State treasuries were empty. A customary lifestyle for the elite needed tending. And the number of mouths to feed was increasing at an alarming rate.[4]

Land – not land itself but the future promise of it – was the way to save the early Republic, to free up commerce and bring prosperity. Without it the United States would not have been able to take its place on the world stage, alongside the Spanish, French and against the British. The situation led to a land mania, financed from Europe as well as the United States, that lined many pockets, and gave rise to many lucrative commercial enterprises.

For a proper rundown on land mania it is well worth reading Michael Blaakman's wonderful writing on the subject.[5] For the purpose of introducing Colt's world, it is enough to sketch a brief picture of the world and language of late eighteenth-century land. And the language used to 'sell' land as a commodity, the

---

[4] Taylor, A. (2001) *American Colonies: The Settling of North America*, New York: Viking Penguin; Taylor, A. (2016) *American Revolutions: A Continental History, 1750–1804*, New York: Norton; Taylor. A. (1996) *William Cooper's Town: Power and Persuasion on the Frontier of the Early American Republic*, New York: Vintage; Taylor, A. (2006) *The Divided Ground: Indians, Settlers, and the Northern Borderland of the American Revolution*, New York: Knopf. See also Nye, D. (2003) *America as Second Creation: Technology and Narratives of New Beginnings*, Cambridge: MIT Press.

[5] Blaakman, M. (2016) 'Speculation nation: Land and mania in the Revolutionary American Republic, 1776–1803', PhD thesis, Yale; to be published as Blaakman, M. (forthcoming) *Speculation Nation: Land Mania in the Revolutionary American Republic* (Philadelphia: University of Pennsylvania Press); Winchester, S. (2013) *The Men Who United the States* London: William Collins; Linklater, A. (2015) *Owning the Earth: The Transforming History of Land Ownership*, London: Bloomsbury.

selling of the dream – of a new land, forged in the wilderness, of equality, of yeoman farmers with equal-sized plots laid out grid-wise in an agrarian economy of true democracy. This was President Thomas Jefferson's vision for the new Republic. The dream has carried on to this day in the United States, despite evidence to undermine it throughout the centuries.

This dream – this myth – was assumed by many to have happened – at least for a time – in the frontier settlements. It was of course always at the expense of the existing inhabitants. Historians have an increasingly uncomfortable recognition that Native American societies that were supplanted by the new frontier settler colonials from the 1780s onwards were themselves highly respectable civilisations pretty brutally displaced, cheated, by the Anglo-Americans. It seems unthinkable to my own generation, so captivated by those societies who maintained a light touch on the landscape, that a civilised, settled nation of villagers should be ripped from their lands, and penned into rectangular tracts drawn (reservations) on a map before they were laid out on the land. Penned, in both senses of the word, within the rectangular plots (plotted by the pristine new liberated individual states), the Native Americans were written about, and written to, in such a way that their access to 'rights' as 'people' ebbed away. The treaties and contracts were dressed up with legality but essentially were hollow gestures. The word 'treaty' covered a whole ragbag of hoodwinking sessions, bribes, 'contract' exchanges – between one or more Native American nations, or parts of nations, with states, the United States, or speculators large or small. The key ones mentioned by Colt, which took place at Canandaigua in 1789 and 1794, are a mixture – 1789 setting out an annual 'annuity' and 1794 making a formal treaty.

But once Native American 'rights' had been eroded, the states began to apportion, claim, and sell land which most people had never set eyes on. For each state, and for the United States as a whole, the 1783 Treaty of Paris started a land rush, a land bubble. The land to the west of what the British had called the

Proclamation Line had belonged to the Native Americans under law until 1783. Now it was open to white settlement. Blaakman tells the story of that settlement in several states, including New York and Pennsylvania, where Colt settled. Things progressed slightly differently and in slightly different time scales in these states, but the result was broadly the same. These states professed a bias against big speculating land companies, and in favour of individual settlers who would by hard work cut down trees and plough their new farms. But in both states 'land' was sold quickly to land companies as well as to individuals, in large quantities to fill State coffers – even if it was with IOUs and repayment terms, it allowed the State to get on with necessary business. This was long before the land had even been mapped, in rectangles of land marked out as 'townships'. What was sold were 'warrants'. The political discourse insisted these warrants were sold or given to individuals, but the reality was quite different.

In New York State, where Judah Colt first settled (1789-96), warrants were given in the 1780s to discharged soldiers, who often sold them on to others. They were also sold legally to big speculators: a large tract was sold to Oliver Phelps and Stephen Gorham, who were to play a big part in Colt's story and who set up land offices both on the frontier and back in Suffield, Mass., where they sold warrants on to settlers, or would-be settlers – or individuals who bought them to sell again (flippers is a term used for the latter group). The warrants themselves might not be paid for until they were sold again – or they might be sold on 'terms' with interest over a number of years.

Large amounts of these land transactions stayed in their paper or warrant form for many years. Colt still had some in this form in his 1832 will. Just pieces of paper. Though by this time they will have been mapped, parcels of rough forest adjacent to farms. Once a warrant came into the hand of a would-be settler, he had the task of beginning to clear the land, farm it, build on it, and claim his right to the land deeds from the State. Even then he might not own the property outright; he might have had to take the land on 'terms'. Harm Jan Huidekoper reveals just how expensive the task of becoming a western frontier farmer could be, as he explains in his autobiography why he decided to go into the business of land speculation first in New York State as an employee, rather than simply buy land:

> I have since often smiled at the erroneous idea, which I, as well as numerous other Europeans, entertained on this subject. In Europe, the man who owns a hundred acres of good land is rich, and can draw from it more than a competency with little more labour than that of superintending the cultivation of it. Now Europeans are apt to connect the same ideas with the possession of land in this Country; and as they hear that very good land is to be had here at from two to four dollars per acre, they are led to believe that it requires but a few hundred dollars to make a man independent for life. I need not add that when I saw my friend de Clercq's farm covered with stumps, it did not exactly realise the beau ideal which I had formed to myself of a territorial possession; and when I learned afterwards that it had taken about $4,000 to make his farm what it was, I became sensible, that I was not rich enough to become a farmer.[6]

In Pennsylvania, where Colt subsequently settled (1796-1832), the ideal of a yeoman farmers' democracy chimed with the Quaker ideals still strong in government. The land laws here initially laid down that each tract should belong to an individual. This meant paper warrants were given to individual soldiers in lieu of pay, and were meant to be given directly to individual aspiring farmers. However, from the beginning this law was flouted. Land would be 'notionally' held by lots of different people, while actually held by a company. The case of the Pennsylvania Population Company (which was to play a big part in Colt's story) illustrates this well. In 1792 Pennsylvania bought from the Federal government the last piece of Pennsylvania, a

---

[6] Tiffany, N.M. and F. (1904), *Harm Jan Huidekoper*, Cambridge: Riverside Press, p. 47.

triangle (the Erie Triangle) whose long side was formed by the lake shoreline, giving lake access.[7] The same year the Pennsylvania Population Company (PPC) was established and began to acquire land in the Triangle. The company got round State rules on ownership by buying the land in the names of individuals connected to its directors. The chief director of the company, John Nicholson, had been State Comptroller General (1782–94), although at the same time a great entrepreneur in mining, flour, an ironmonger, a philanthropist and a builder of roads and canals. When the PPC was set up, most of the land, located almost entirely in the Erie Triangle by Lake Erie, was bought by Nicholson. He seems to have used his State office 'to pre-empt' the entire area as soon as the land was offered for sale. He confessed later to having 'borrowed names' to make this happen.

The Pennsylvania State legislature, however, passed laws in 1792 that were inconvenient for the land companies, big and small. A tract of land could not be owned by an 'alien' (a non-US citizen). After two years the would-be owner had to have a dwelling house erected and four acres cleared, and had then to prove they had lived on the plot continuously for five years. This led to the confusion and law suits that Colt was left to deal with as best he could from 1797 onwards, as agent of the PPC. A 1794 law increased the tangle, by allowing the clause about living continuously for five years to be relaxed in the case of threat of Indian invasion. Small companies and individuals used this clause to take possession of tracts and contest their ownership.

All these individual State differences, the twists and turns of the Federal and State legislatures, helped make individual fortunes, and also break them. But the primary purpose, for the new Republic, was fulfilled. The states received some much needed cash – and a quantity of promise notes.

---

[7] Hale, R. N. (1949) 'The Pennsylvania Population Company', *Pennsylvania History*, 16 (2), pp. 122–30; Arbuckle, R. (1974) 'John Nicholson & the Pennsylvania Population Company', *Western Pennsylvania Historical Magazine*, 57 (4), pp. 353–5.

What happened in Pennsylvania is summed up by the Bucks in their 1949 book, *The Planting of Civilisation in Western Pennsylvania*: 'The land system of the state was a shifting compromise that satisfied no-one, brought in little revenue, ruined most of the speculators, and delayed settlement.'[8] But there were many who did benefit, Colt amongst them.

The commodification of land on such a grand scale spawned a host of other money-making opportunities. Not just the large land companies, but even the small hoped to make money in this early version of 'futures'. A host of Colt's contemporaries found ways to climb the social ladder – in fact the small men, the little fish in the big pond, seem to have fared better than their more sophisticated cosmopolitan grand-scale speculators, whose fortunes were more precarious – Phelps, Burr, Nicholson, all big names in Colt's story, gained and then lost wealth. The stories of these smaller men are being told. Marcus Gallo has told the story of John Adlum, who made a comfortable fortune in western Pennsylvania like Colt, and Alan Taylor gave us the glorious story of Cooperstown.[9]

So were 'surveyors' of land; a host of jobs mushroomed for the State and for land companies big and small. Any bright man, a little knowledgeable in geometry, trigonometry and maths, and armed with the equipment – a Jacob's staff and a chain – could make a good living. A Jacob's staff had been used to survey the heavens in medieval times, but during the eighteenth century it was used for the more earthbound purpose of measuring land – for ownership. The term 'Jacob's staff' – which would have been familiar to Colt – gives land surveying a Biblical blessing – no pillage of the land, instead a sacred undertaking. The surveyor's

---

[8] Buck, S. and Buck, E. (1949) *The Planting of Civilization in Western Pennsylvania*, Pittsburgh: University of Pittsburgh Press, p. 205.

[9] Taylor, A. (1996) *William Cooper's Town: Power and Persuasion on the Frontier of the Early American Republic*, New York: Vintage; Gallo, M. (2018), 'Improving independence: The struggle over land surveys in Northwestern Pennsylvania in 1794', *Pennsylvania Magazine of History and Biography* 142 (2), pp. 131–61.

tools themselves were in high demand – steel or brass chains, pegs, theodolites, rings – Gibson's handy book on practical surveying, in its eighth edition in 1798 specifically published for the new Republic, lists all these necessary items.[10]

And although many of the instruments were manufactured still in Europe, there were new makers in Connecticut, in New York, in Philadelphia; the entire new country was helping the growth of the Republic's economy.

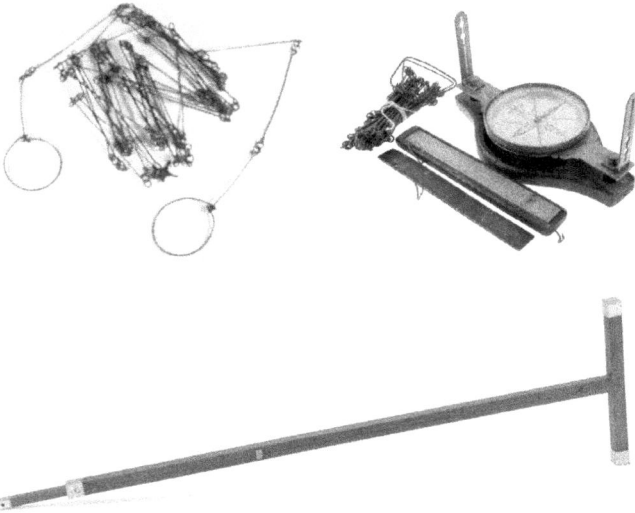

Figures 5-7: Surveyor's tools: chain (Gunther's chain), compass, and slide rule for calculations; and Jacob's staff. All of these would have been part of Colt's surveying equipment.[11]

---

[10] Gibson, R. (1798) *A Treatise of practical surveying; which is demonstrated from its first principles: Wherein everything that is useful and curious in that art, is fully considered & explained*, New York: William A. Davis & Co.

[11] https://www.colonialsense.com/Society/SotT/GChain/chain2.jpg https://www.amphilsoc.org/blog/few-technical-items-questions-about-18th-century-surveying-instruments-answered-part-ii https://en.wikipedia.org/wiki/Jacob%27s_staff#/media/File:Bastone_di _Giacobbe_inv_3167_IF_46850.jpg, downloaded 20 November 2020.

As David Nye laid out in his brilliant book *America as Second Creation*, the land mania of the late eighteenth century kick-started a whole lot of industries. Making the machinery for mills – grist and saw mills. The axles for waggons. The ploughs and spades, axes and cauldrons needed in the settler colonial land. Digging the quarries for the road stone. Making the boats and ships to sail goods up-country. Constructing sturdy containers for the journeys.[12]

The industrial boom of the first half of the nineteenth century, the water-powered mills for cotton, the manufacture of houseware, farming and dairy implements – all took off at this time.

And a final word on the abiding myth of the 'manifest destiny' of the population of the United States. Historians have been writing about the early frontier since it was first laid out at speed in the 1780s and 90s. From the beginning the 'Early Pioneers' have been revered. In the first place it was a way of finally staking claim to this land which was not theirs to take. The first fathers of a town (like Colt and many others I name below) wrote their own biographies; this was followed a generation later by 'memories' of old people, quaint tales of frontier life – women who made the butter on the waggons as they rolled westward, men (and women) who stood up to the marauding Indian, dances and barn raisings on the new country. I've used quotes from these below – you'll find the references to them. My own ancestors wrote two such books about Erie.[13] Implicitly, these books give those ancestors the right to be there, on that land, settler colonial-style, bringing their way of life with them. At the turn of the twentieth century, there was a re-evaluation – Jackson Turner invented the term 'manifest destiny' of the United States explicitly – with an explicit warning that land was running out – the Pacific had been reached – and an implicit

---

12 Nye, D. (2003), op. cit.

13 Spencer, H.R. (1962) *Erie: A History*, private publication; Sanford, L.G. (1861), *The History of Erie County, Pennsylvania*, Philadelphia: J.B. Lippincott & Co., enlarged and privately printed, 1894.

meaning that US citizens and US business had a right to global supremacy, just as the early pioneers had the right to Native American territory.[14]

Scholarship in the mid-twentieth century tried a more nuanced approach – The Bucks' book on planting civilisation in western Pennsylvania displays its prejudice in its title, but it gives a credible, if idealised, detailed account of building the communities west of the Alleghenies. It still covers up the enduring Native American story, and still suggests these settler communities were at their outset equal, only becoming socially stratified later.[15]

But it is not until the turn of the twenty-first century that a sober evaluation of what happened began in earnest. Historians then explored full wanton destruction of a way of life – and countless communities – of First Nation people who were co-existing and co-adapting to life alongside the early trappers and missionaries. They mapped the power of early capital. They began to explore the lives of women, slaves, indentured workers, and Native Americans on the frontier. They began to show how quickly the Anglo American communities grew in western New York and western Pennsylvania, and how closely they followed the contours of society on the eastern seaboard, which in many ways was unchanged from colonial days.[16]

Colt's diaries allow us to explore this version of events in some detail. His education was English, to the core. His upbringing ensured Native Americans and slaves were invisible – as much as they could be. He was determined to climb the social ladder, and did so very easily in his first frontier years, earning the right to the title 'esquire'.

Colt shows the steps of his climb, through his *Journal* and *Narrative*. These steps are complicated; they involve a lot of

[14] Turner, F.J. (1921) *The Frontier in American History*, New York: H. Holt and Co.

[15] Buck, S. and E. (1949).

[16] Taylor, A. *American Revolutions*, op. cit.; Blaakman, M., op. cit.

buying and selling – of goods and of promises in the shape of land warrants – and travel. Buzzing back and forth from the frontier to New England, to New York, to Philadelphia, he became commissioned salesman, purchaser, farmer, merchant, logistics manager, storekeeper, land agent, gent. All at the same time.

Almost more important than the rest, a close reading of the words themselves reveals how language can be used to obscure uncomfortable subjects, and highlight others favourably. Colt reveals his aspirations through what he writes about (and what he omits), and through the words he uses. To give an example: Once Colt reaches the Erie Triangle and starts to have trouble with Irish settlers, whom he labels 'adverse' settlers, he often starts a journal entry by describing the weather as grey and threatening – using the term 'Lowry' to make his point. His chief 'adverse settlers' were from a large Irish family who had arrived in Philadelphia before the Revolution without any money – their name was 'Lowry'. A close reading of the words of the diaries reveals the aspirations of a man such as Colt. In this kind of reading we discover the spirit of both the man and his times.

Chapter 2

Childhood and youth, 1761–85

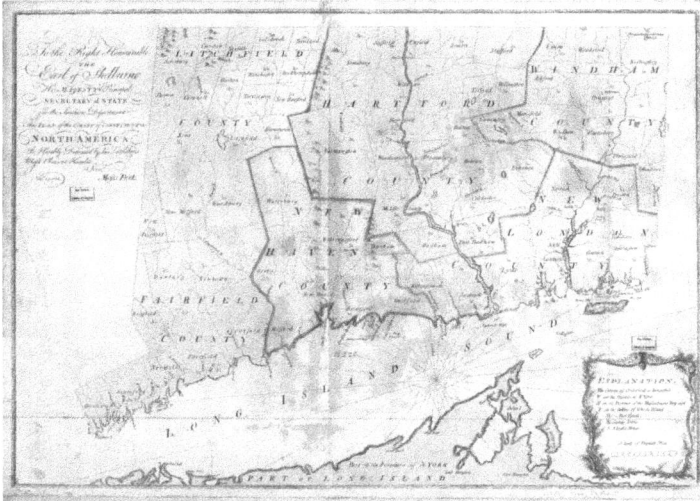

Figure 8: 'To the right honourable, the Earl of Shelbourne, His Majesty's principal Secretary of State for the Southern Department. This plan of the colony of Connecticut in North-America' (1766).[17] Colt (born 1761) grew up in New London County at the mouth of the Connecticut River, right of centre.

To begin in Old Lyme in 1760s Connecticut, at the mouth of the wide Connecticut River. The houses pictured are on the main streets of Old Lyme; Colt's family farm would not have been this elegant, but they would have given him a taste of what he might aspire to. The first house was just across from the Congregational

---

[17] https://www.loc.gov/item/73691553/, downloaded 19 November 2020.

Church where Colt's father was a deacon. It was built in 1700 by Amos Tinker and bought in 1753 by Jim McCurdy, a Scotch Irish merchant who arrived in Connecticut from the old country, and built a fortune from shipping. McCurdy was a Patriot in the War of Independence, and had George Washington to stay in April 1776, and Lafayette in 1778.

Figures 9–11: Houses in Old Lyme, from the time of Colt's childhood.[18]

The second house pictured was built when Colt was in his early twenties by Samuel Mather, a sea captain who became a wealthy merchant through his trade with the West Indies. The

---

[18] http://historicbuildingsct.com/the-john-mccurdy-house-1700/
http://historicbuildingsct.com/the-capt-samuel-mather-house-1790/
http://historicbuildingsct.com/justin-smith-house-1710/, downloaded 5 June 2020.

smaller third house – probably nearer to the size of the Colt farm – was built in 1710 and belonged the Mathers, the Tinkers and the Smiths during the eighteenth century.

Southern New England society, 1760s–80s: Trading, manufacture and consumerism

Colt was born in 1761 not far from Old Lyme, into the family of a small farmer, a dean of the local church. Joseph and Desiree (née Pratt) Colt had eight children: Isaiah, born in 1757, who died of smallpox in 1777, Deborah, born 1759, Judah 1761, followed by Desiree 1763, Assenath 1764, Joseph 1766, Samuel 1771, Jabez 1772. Quite a household! But usual for that time.

In his childhood, Old Lyme was a busy seaport, in the shadow of nearby New London where boats took cargo of salt fish and local manufactures south to the Carolinas and the Caribbean, and east over the Atlantic to Europe. The port also handled the increasing trade in commodities – glass, china, furniture, carpets, material – from the Old World, and cargoes of lemons, tea, – anything which could be sold to the increasing numbers of well-to-do New Englanders. The houses of the rich – their wealth from shipping, merchandise or, increasingly, western land speculation – were smart, clapperboard houses, two-storey, with a grand front door and often nine windows at the front, window glass imported, polished planed floors of wood, fine furniture and carpets. The poor of Lyme – labourers, servants – were a mixture of poor white families, and 'coloureds' who, in the local census of 1764– 5, included the categories Indian, Mulatto, and Black.

There were mills, ferries, chandlers, general stores, lawyers, smithies, woodworkers, corn merchants, haberdashers, printers, and churches. There were carters and pedlars – Native Americans selling baskets, spoons, fish, Indian ornaments. There were militia on the streets, especially in the 1770s and 80s, and town meetings full of the urgent business of the Revolution.

The schools were for white boys only. Girls' education, if any, was at home. And the learning of the poor and 'coloured', including the Native Americans, was, likewise, haphazard. The boys' schools were seasonal, for the winter months only. They used English primers, teaching arithmetic, writing, reading, and a little history and geography. The teachers were for the most part young men on their way to college, to become lawyers or physicians. If this was to be their career, they went on from the common English school to a grammar school. Colt took this path, which must have cost his father dear, but there seems to have been no thought of him going on to college. However, he did teach in Common English schools in local communities – in Old Saybrook (1782), North Quarter of Lyme (1783), and Old Society of Lyme (1784), in the winters until he was 23, and he went on teaching after he left Lyme, in Edington, North Carolina (1785), and Williamstown, Massachusetts (1786).

British values at school

Colt's grammar school education will have included Greek, Latin, English literature (poetry, plays, novels), history and geography, as well as ethics and rhetoric and some more advanced mathematics.[19] It is entirely possible – though he never tells us this – that he learnt more vocational skills as well. (Also in the 1780s, private academies were set up teaching bookkeeping, surveying, and other skills that were needed in the new Republic.) Colt's education shaped his early world view, the moral compass and outlook on which his future life was grounded. A very British compass, class-based, looking up to classical learning, the professions, the church and life as a 'landed' gentleman. All delivered within a resilient colonial setting – chafing under the taxation of the mother country but made in its mould.

---

[19] Middlekauff, R. (1961) 'A persistent tradition: The classical curriculum in eighteenth-century New England', *The William and Mary Quarterly* 18 (1), pp. 54–67.

Native Americans rendered invisible

Another extremely important early influence – crucial for any settler colonist – is the ability to render invisible the first, now supplanted, nation. Recent work by Mancini[20] has shown us that, far from disappearing from the landscape, or conveniently keeping to their 'reservations', the ousted and conquered American peoples were still there – in plain sight. In the second half of the nineteenth century, southern Connecticut undertook censuses, some at the request of the English Crown, some for the State. There are also records of land disputes, and land ownership, as well as lists of different trades – including seamen, agricultural labourers and servants. While some of the material may lack accuracy, it begins to make visible what was, in the gaze of Colt's contemporaries, almost invisible. In 1782, reporting on the current status of the Indian population in southern New England, J. Hector St. John de Crèvecoeur, in *Letters from an American Farmer*, informed a broad audience of European and American readers that among the Indian tribes of southern New England, were the

> Mohiguinen, Pequots, Narraganets, Niantics, Massachusetts, Wampanoags, Nipnets ... They are gone, and every memorial of them is lost; no vestiges whatever are left of those swarms which once inhabited this country.... They have all disappeared either in the wars which the Europeans carried on against them, or else they have mouldered away, gathering in some of their ancient towns, in contempt and oblivion.[21]

---

[20] Mancini, J.R. (2009) 'Beyond reservation: Indian survivance in southern New England and eastern Long Island, 1713–1861', PhD thesis, University of Connecticut; Mancini, J.R. (2015) 'In contempt and oblivion: Censuses, ethno geography, and hidden Indian histories in eighteenth-century southern New England', Mashantucket Pequot Museum and Research Center, *Ethnohistory*, 62 (1), pp. 61–94.

[21] Mancini, J.R. (2015), p. 61.

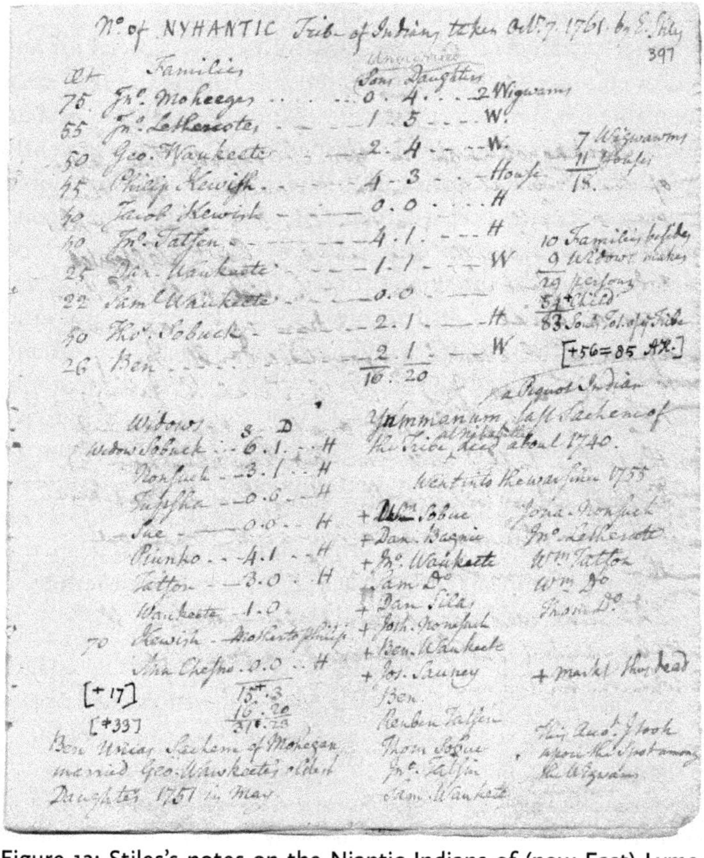

Figure 12: Stiles's notes on the Niantic Indians of (now East) Lyme, Connecticut. There was academic interest in what was happening to the Native Americans, even in colonial times; as Stiles's work shows, they were living on the margins of the society Colt was raised in.

In East Lyme, in the autumn of Judah Colt's birth in 1761, E. Stiles compiled a list[22] of the Niantic ('Nyhantic') tribe which demonstrates their presence – 85 souls, of

[22] Stiles's papers, 7 October 1761, 1: 397, quoted in Mancini, J.R. (2009), p. 71.

34

whom 54 were children, living in houses and wigwams.

There were also groups in towns, and in adjacent farms, not on the reservations but instead mixed in with village communities. On the eve of the Revolution, Mancini tells us, less than 50 per cent of Native Americans lived on reservations – and these are the ones who were counted. The census figures seem to have been partial, often only counting white householders.[23]

Increasingly, too, as black freed slaves and those children of mixed ancestry, then called 'mulatto', increased in number, all, including Native Americans, were listed together by the white town administrators as 'coloured'. Many men from these communities enlisted in the eighteenth-century wars – including the War of Independence – in which they died in disproportionate numbers, leaving destitute widows and children for the various Connecticut authorities to support. There are enough stories of pedlars – such as Ann Wampy, the basket seller, who took her stock of baskets on the road[24] – and records of land disputes, and of seamen, for us to build a picture of an economy relying on the fast assimilating Native Americans – not a community where these people had died out, as is assumed, but one in which they had adapted to survive, as a conquered and displaced culture. By the late eighteenth century, the Native Americans – members of the First Nation – are not described, and probably not even seen, as people – the women are described as 'squaws' and the men as 'Indians'. In a case taken to the English crown courts in 1770, a lawyer describes dealing with the Native Americans whose land he wishes to possess, maintaining that, like wild animals, they had no rights to land:

> When the English Treated with them it was not as with Independent States (for they had no such thing as a Civil Polity...) but as with savages, whom they were to quiet & manage as well as they could, sometimes by flattery, but oftener by force – Who

---

[23] Mancini, J. (2015), op. cit.

[24] Mancini, J. (2009), p. 142.

would not treat a Company of Lyons Wolves or Bears (whom the Indians but too nearly resemble) if he saw himself surrounded by [them] ready to fall upon him, & even call them Friends & Allies too, if he thought it would for a Moment repress their Rage, & give him time to take measures for his security.[25]

This dual construction – of the 'Indian' as alien, other, threatening; and the Indian as invisible, though vital contributor to the economy and the State as soldier, labourer, servant, pedlar – was to be extremely useful to Colt in the years to come. He played a part in the brutal displacement of the Native Americans living west of the mountains, who in the early eighteenth century had been promised a peaceful co-existence by the British, only to be swept from their villages into camps, and reservations, or marginalised in the towns as they had been in Lyme.[26] But though he was part of this violation, he could ignore it, sweep it aside – precisely because it echoed civil society in the Connecticut of his youth. We know that Colt, for the rest of his life, will have had contact with Native Americans; that they offered him shelter, and probably offered him medicine and food. Yet the formal accounts of the First Nation in his *Narrative* and *Journal* are of a population in abject poverty, starving, who come to a 'set-piece' encounter with the large-scale land speculators Phelps and Gorham in New York State in 1789 and appear later, as an ancient people, long gone, in the 'Erie Triangle', when he intervened to stop new farmers digging up an Indian burial ground.[27] A very comfortable act of deference to a people he helped to displace.

[25] Den Ouden, A.E. (2001) 'Against conquest: Land, culture, and power in the eighteenth-century histories of the native peoples of Connecticut', dissertation, University of Connecticut, p. 263.

[26] Buck, S. and E. (1949), p. 96.

[27] Sanford, L.G. (1894), *History of Erie County, Pennsylvania*, p. 22.

Others who go unmentioned in Colt's *Narrative*

It would be wrong to leave the invisibility of the Native Americans in Colt's *Narrative* without a mention of the equally invisible slaves and women, whether coloured or not. Connecticut newspapers of these years have advertisements for slave sales – and rewards were offered for runaway slaves. Better-off households in New England at this period often contained slaves, and indentured servants. One of the very few mentioned by Colt is a slave girl called Chloe – a mulatto – whom he took to help with his household, when he moved from Canandaigua to Erie County, Pennsylvania; she had originally come from his father's farm in Lyme. On 25 January 1802 he records: 'requested of Joseph [Colt] to purchase Cloe, a mellato girl being with Moses Sill if to be bought on reasonable terms, and advise me thereof.' Chloe's further indenture is described later in this text.

White women appear as mothers, sisters and wives throughout Colt's *Narrative*. But their agency, as dairy managers, gardeners, bakers, food conservers, cooks, household managers, goes unsung. This lacuna in Colt's tale becomes even more stark the further he journeys west, in the two new communities he had a hand in raising. Colt's wife Elizabeth, as we will see, is seen by him as his religious guide, and revered as the mother of his children (only one of whom survived very early infancy, and then only until five years old) but she is otherwise rarely mentioned.

Colt's own *Narrative* gives us only half a page on his childhood:

From the time of my birth until I arrived at the age of twenty-three years I resided the greater part of my time in my father's family, assisting him in working his farm from Spring until Fall, and in the Winter months was sent to the common English and Grammar School, where I learnt reading writing and arithmetic, and having made considerable proficiency in these branches, I taught a school during the winter of 1782 at Saybrook, North Society, in the Winter of 1783 in the North Quarter of Lyme,[&] in the winter of 1784 in the Old Society of Lyme.[28]

[28] See 'Principal sources'.

The fettering hand of British colonial rule

It is astonishing that the momentous events of Colt's childhood in New England are not mentioned. Where are the reports of pre-revolutionary discontent with the British? Where are the reports of the troops in Old Lyme? Where the sounds of battle? Of the naval encounters? Were the events too recent, too painful, too commonplace to mention at the time of writing in the early nineteenth century? This seems unlikely.

Discontent with British rule was widespread in southern New England in the 1760s and 70s of Colt's childhood – and his early manhood saw the conflict erupt. Lyme, like other towns, had its meetings, its rallies, its calls to arms. Being on the seaboard, it saw troop movement, naval engagement, soldiers leaving for the front and returning, wounded or otherwise. But there is no mention of this in Colt's *Narrative*.

Why does he not mention the Declaration of Independence? Or the War of Independence? The Loyalists and the Patriots? Many men in Lyme had fought for independence from the British from the 1770s onwards. His sisters married men who had fought in the war. He subsequently did business with and sold land to people who had made fortunes in the war, or had had a glorious war which they continued to boast about. He keeps quiet. He was teaching school when he could have been in the militia. He had an older brother who died of smallpox in the years of the war – had this brother enlisted? Had his mother and father pleaded for him not to do the same? Was someone needed to stay to work the farm? Had the whole family been quietly pro-loyalist, obliged to adapt to Patriotism after the peace was signed? Colt's wife was the daughter of a captain on the American side, so it seems unlikely that he himself was a loyalist, though many who had been loyalists simply adapted to the new government.

Possibly the answer lies in the aftermath of the war, in the early years of the thirteen United States. There may have been discrimination on a local level – we can only suspect there was – but the general rule seems to have been that the families who stayed on after the British defeat, and showed themselves loyal to the new Republic, were simply left to get on with life. There seems to have been no especial shaming of people who had sympathised with the British, or hadn't been involved, and who stayed in the new Republic, as the following suggests:[29]

> It would be of no service now to draw out of oblivion the names of individuals who at various times during the eight years of darkness and conflict were suspected of being inimical to the liberties of their country. Many of these changed their sentiments and came over to the side of independence, and all at last acquiesced in their own happiness and good fortune, growing out of the emancipation of their country from a foreign scepter. It is an easier as well as more pleasing task to mention names that, on account of voluntary activity, sacrifice of personal interest, and deeds of valorous enterprise, exerted for the rights of man, lie prominent upon the surface, illuminating the whole period by their brightness.

If Colt and his family had sided with the British in the eight dark years, it might have given Colt and his brothers an added reason for leaving the neighbourhood, and would certainly explain his hurried and rather sparse description of his childhood.

Piecing together what we know of the society Colt was brought up in, it seems that Connecticut made him who he was, gave him his moral compass. One in which wealth was sought after, social hierarchy predominated, trade and its trappings flourished, English culture prevailed, and white Anglo American men were at the top of the heap. Viewed like this, Connecticut may have lived through eight years of darkness, but it came out the other side with a value system largely intact. As we move forward in Colt's life, it is worth remembering that he continued

---

[29] Hurd, D.H, (1882) *History of New London County, Connecticut, with Biographical Sketches of Many of Its Pioneers and Prominent Men*, Philadelphia: J.B. Lippincott & Co.

almost every year to visit his Connecticut family – often for months at a time. He 'renewed his acquaintance' more than once each visit.

Colt finished his period as a schoolteacher in Connecticut in 1784. He was restless, as he remembered it when he wrote his *Narrative*, and wanted to 'become acquainted with the world'.[30] He 'obtained the consent of my parents to let me make a Voige to the South, and accordingly on the 15th day of November 1784, took passage in the sloop "Betsy" (Elnathan Hatch Master) for North Carolina and sailed the same day'. Elnathan Hatch was a local captain who had been in the revolutionary wars, his ship had also known revolutionary service. There are a few tantalizing glimpses of him through naval and State records. He was described in 1782 as age 35, 5 foot 8 inches tall, with a dark complexion, blue eyes and black hair. At that time, two years before his voyage with Colt, he was first lieutenant on the Connecticut privateer *Brigantine*.

All we can deduce from the following year's (1785) adventures – which included a shipwreck on Bermuda, and teaching school in North Carolina – is that after them he firmly changed tack. The sea captains, the international merchants, who may have provided early role models for the aspiring boy – he turned his back on them. Instead he looked to a modern, contemporary way to make his fortune. He made more plans to travel, but this time inland.

---

[30] *Narrative*, author's collection, p. 1.

Chapter 3

Colt starts on his move westwards

Still restless, Colt went with his uncle Harris Colt to see a plot his father and uncle wanted to view in the North country, up in the new State of Vermont, a plot 'of which he is an agent and my father a small shareholder' (*Narrative*). Land speculation was already, in the 1780s, one stream of potential income for people in his home town, as sketched out above. Note the terms 'agent' and 'small shareholder' in his *Narrative*. 'Agent' shows Uncle Harris was employed – maybe salaried, more likely on commission – by speculators, 'capitalists' who had bought the land on spec., and wanted to get on with selling it. 'Small shareholder' shows us his father had shares in the company employing Harris. There is no suggestion that either Colt's uncle or his father were would-be settlers. And the situation they found on arrival – that the land was yet to be 'run off by the State Surveyor General' – this was again a situation that would have been familiar to Colt's contemporaries, and needed no explanation. Land as we've seen above, could be sold notionally long before it was marked out on the ground ready for settlement. The land 'could not be subdivided into lots as was our intention to do'. This was a common setback of the period. Making a fortune out of land was not at all straightforward. The older Colt men turned back home. They didn't continue with their mission because there would have been no point – no money to be made – yet.

They would have subdivided the plot if it had already been 'run off', surveyed and marked it out, ready for further sales back home – which would have represented a sound investment for the family.

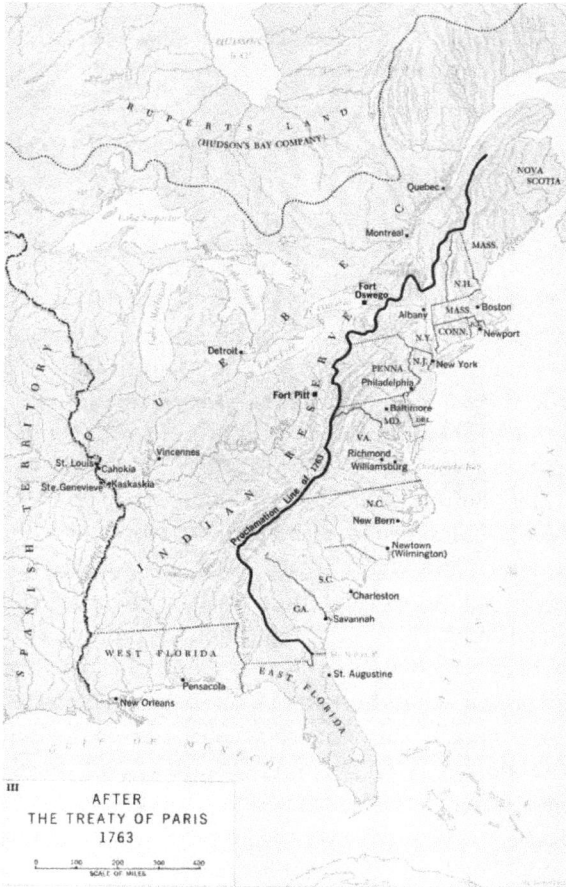

Figure 13: This modern map of the 1763 Proclamation Line shows clearly the King's decision to reserve lands to the west of the line to the Native Americans, and keep the colonists out. (Further west at the time was 'Spanish territory'.) The line was withdrawn in the 1783 Treaty of Paris, which allowed the new United States access to the West.[31]

---

[31] http://www.emersonkent.com/map_archive/north_america_1763_proclamation.htm, downloaded 20 November 2020.

The fact that Colt records this episode suggests that he might have expected sympathy from his early nineteenth-century audience – this was a setback they could sympathise with, understand. He records that he stayed on in the region, then frontier country, while his older relatives went back to Connecticut. He is projecting his reader forward into his future – a reader who would have been likely to know his history in land speculation, and have shared in the images of wealth and influence this conjured up. His uncle had been a land agent – why not him too?

Several key factors help us understand why land speculation might have been an attractive gamble for Harris and Joseph Colt, and for Colt himself. Some have been described above. One – absolutely crucial – after the War of Independence, and especially after the settlement with the British in 1783 in Paris, was that the former British lands to the American West were no longer bound into a British-Indian treaty. The so-called 'Proclamation Line' of 1763, beyond which settlement was forbidden, was done away with in Paris. The traditional pattern, where trappers and hunters settled in the lands beyond the mountains alongside the Native American villages and towns, trading with them, and with the merchants who took the goods to the East and from there to Europe – all that was gone. That society – of which we get a glimpse when Judah Colt initially goes west – was fairly mutually tolerant, and mutually dependent. The early eighteenth-century Native American villages had evolved to become more dependent on trading with the white merchants by that time, and they had started to adopt some of the settlers' farming methods. They kept some livestock and grew crops the New England colonists had imported from Europe – wheat, oats, and so on – in addition to their own traditional crops of pumpkin, corn, beans and potatoes.

There had also been some intermingling, in this western territory, with Native American children schooled by missionaries, or individual white families. The areas to the north and west of the Proclamation Line were well and quite thickly settled with villages and towns, with a sizeable population of Native American communities. (Here I resist the use of the English word 'tribe' because of the heavy connotations of some lesser existence.) But as we've seen, post-1776, things changed. Initially the colonists fought the British and Native Americans on this western soil and won, leaving devastation – and starving Native American villagers – as they went. Then, rapidly after 1783, the Federal government and its constituent States took, bought, or leased large tracts of land from the Native Americans, which they sold on to land companies, or individuals, or gave in lieu of pay to Patriotic troops. The land opened up for settler-colonisers. The race for profit was on.

As Michael Blaakman tells us in his compelling work on 'land mania',[32] this resulted in the States producing slips of paper, which signified plots of as yet un-surveyed land, as currency, and this was the way the new nation's economy survived and expanded. This was an early gamble on future markets. War debts drove the westward expansion.

The New England population had increased up to seven-fold in some places, and this made farms too small to support these big families. Buying land (now scarce) had become extremely expensive within the settlements, too, so sons and daughters could not simply start married life on a farm near to their families. They had to contemplate moving. We know from Colt's own experience that his farm was too small for all the eight siblings – that his father suggested a subdivision of the land that was not enough to attract Colt – and that, furthermore, there had been a terrible harvest due to the ravages of the Hessian fly (1788) which served to underline the precariousness of a livelihood based on farming a small acreage in southern Connecticut. In the end, all four Colt brothers moved west, though not just as farmers.

---

[32] Blaakman, M. (2016).

There was an urgent need for good farmland in the early Republic. But also, Europe was itself experiencing an exodus. Political upheavals, bad harvests, and population growth drove some people into towns, but others across the ocean to the Americas, chasing the promise of new cheap and good land.

The imperative to move to find land was already in train before the Revolution – in fact it was almost certainly one of the reasons for the move to independence. So a political and in the event military solution was needed – to cast off British rule. As Andro Linklater puts it:

> Attracted by the prospect of owning land outright, almost one hundred thousand immigrants from Ulster and Germany, augmented by 180,000 free individuals from Britain, together with sixty thousand indentured servants and criminals, came to America. But natural increase accounted for much of the growth, especially in New England, where large families – six to eight surviving children were common – pushed a population of twenty thousand inhabitants in the mid-seventeenth century to more than four-hundred thousand by the 1750s.[33]

Linklater shows that if property was crucial to the pre-revolutionary American colonies, it was even more crucial in the post-revolutionary era.[34]

Like Britain at that time, New England was becoming increasingly a consumer society. It had turned into one of the sources of irritation with British rule – that so many desirable goods had to be purchased from Britain, so many goods were subject to British taxation, so many laws prevented manufacture by and for the American colonists. The British rule of law was strangling the American economy. The American colonists were eager to manufacture goods themselves, and source their own raw materials. After independence they were no longer

---

[33] Linklater, A. (2015), p. 184.

[34] Ibid., p. 186.

constrained by British laws and taxes. US capital could now itself create elegant houses, furniture, vehicles, new and better farm implements, pots and pans. They could source the raw materials – metal, wood from sawmills – and the transportation networks for getting the material to the customer without giving a cut to the British Crown. Mining, quarrying, smelting, finding sources of water power for manufacture and milling – all took off in what David Nye has named the 'second creation'. And the focus of this second creation was the land beyond the mountains, the 'new' land in the West.

Colt's aspirations, as he commits them to paper, were the shared dreams that shaped the new Republic – more and better land, wealth from speculation, manufacture, commerce – and a new society built in the image of the old, but unfettered by British taxes and laws.

On his way back from northern Vermont, after parting company with his father and uncle, Colt took up an offer of teaching school in Williamsburg, Massachusetts. He stayed there until April 1786, when he fell in with a storekeeper, Thomas Shelden, from Lansingburgh, New York, a rapidly expanding town on the route westward for new settlers travelling from New England. Shelden offered him the job of book keeper, which he accepted. Living in Lansingburgh was Colt's first taste of recent settlement:

> An area of hills, forests, and river plains, Lansingburgh is the oldest settled region and the first chartered village in New York's Rensselaer County. Its rich history began with Abraham Jacob Lansing, who, in 1763, established the area that encompasses Lansingburgh on the eastern banks of the historic Hudson River as a 5,000-acre farm. Eight years later, Lansing laid out his land into a square of 2 by 1.5 miles, with 288 building lots, streets, alleys, and an oblong square village green in the center.[35]

The village was only 15 years old when Colt arrived, and was growing rapidly. This was a very different community from his

---

[35] Rittner, D. (1999) *Lansingburgh*, New York: Arcadia Publishing.

childhood Connecticut, and the life seems to have been engaging. Running a dry goods store on the Hudson River where it meets the Mohawk River took Colt to the heart of the westward movement. Everyone who was going to the frontier needed dry goods to set them up – everything from flour to nails needed to be shipped up river. And Lansingburgh at the time was set to be the new city, the gateway to the West after Albany; it was overtaken by Troy later on, but at this point its hopes were high. It was prosperous – prosperous enough to set up a Masonic lodge on 16 August 1787 and a newspaper, the *Northern Centinel*, also in 1787. The contents the newspaper show how Euro-centric life still was in the new Republic, in a burgeoning community:

> It was a weekly publication and the first newspaper printed within the limits of the territory now known as Rensselaer County. Strange as may seem, it did not contain a line of local news except the publishers' announcement to the public. Its contents consisted of several columns of European 'news' three months old, a few brief items regarding events which had occurred nearly a month before in New York, Boston and Philadelphia, some miscellany and five advertisements.[36]

In a dry goods store Colt will have learnt much about the needs of settlers, as they passed through on their way down the Mohawk towards New York State. They will have bought kettles, farming tools, cloth, kitchen utensils, nails, sacking, seeds – and he will have gained a sound knowledge of where best to source these materials, how to deal with store credit, and seek credit with wholesalers. This would be invaluable knowledge for his future. But in the meantime he hadn't quite cut the ties with home, in Lyme. He was now 26, and his father wanted him to come back. Quoting from his *Narrative*:

---

[36] https://en.wikipedia.org/wiki/History_of_Lansingburgh,_New_York, downloaded 8 October 2020.

My Father appeared anxious to have me settle down on part of his farm & become settled, and made me proposals which were such as a kind parent would do, But having seen a better country for obtaining an Estate by Labour, than the one I was raised in, I excused myself from accepting his offer, and gave him such reasons as I considered satisfied him.

He went back to Lansingburgh in June 1787 to work again in dry goods, first for Shelden, and then for Stephen Gorham – a reputable merchant. He was summoned home abruptly in November 1787 – his father had died. The estate was divided among the heirs. In 1788 he went to view a piece of land he 'held in common' with Richard Sill of Albany, who had bought it at a public sale. It didn't suit him – he says he made a short stay in that 'intire new Country' and returned to Lyme, where he stayed with 'Mother, brothers and Sisters, ... in [the] Farming business, settling the affairs of the Estate of my deceased Father, occasionally road [sic] abroad to some of the neighbouring Towns on Parties of Pleasure.' He was not idle that spring. He seems to have put together his handwritten volume on surveying that spring, between March and April, which he kept amongst his papers all his life.[37] In 1789 he set out again for 'another tour westward'. This time he had

> full determination of fixing on some place for permanent settlement; having previous to my setting out shipped some provision, farming utensils, clothing etc. for Albany which were transported by way of New York to Albany. (*Narrative*)

---

[37] See Bibliography.

Chapter 4

'Falling in with Oliver Phelps Esquire and sundry other adventurers'

In the spring of 1789 Colt left his brother Joseph in charge of the family farm. He had made no firm decision on which course westward to take, but was persuaded to go with 'Oliver Phelps Esquire and sundry other adventurers to the Geneseo County'.[38] His choice of companion was to be very important for his future career. Phelps was returning to the 'Geneseo County' to pursue the settlement of this area, which he had recently bought with his partner Gorham. They had bought it from the State of New York, which had in turn bought it from Massachusetts. (After the Declaration of Independence, there was a considerable amount of trade-offs in land west of the old Proclamation Line.)

Like Colt, Phelps was from Connecticut. Now middle-aged, he had made a first fortune by becoming Superintendent of Army Supplies, a 'commissary' in the Continental army. He was a judge, had been a senator in Massachusetts, and hoped to make a second fortune as a land speculator. His finances, though, were in a perilous state by 1789 when he met Colt; he would soon

---

[38] Geneseo, Genesee: variations on a term used for the region Canandaigua is in. Colt often refers to it as Genesee Country, or County. See the map in Figure 23, where Genesee Country is marked. The Genesee River, some way to the west in New York State, flows north to Rochester on Lake Ontario. Geneseo is a town on the Genesee River. To further complicate matters, today Genesee County in New York State is west of the river, and Genesee Township is just over the border in Pennsylvania near the source of the Genesee River. The town of Geneseo in Illinois was founded in 1836 by Congregationalists from Geneseo, New York. The name 'Genesee' comes from Seneca for 'beautiful valley'.

become heavily in debt and be forced to sell his Connecticut mansion in Suffield. Michael Blaakman has given a vivid account of Phelps as an example of how land mania could lead men into dreams of enormous wealth – only to have them dashed by market failures, problems on the ground, problems at law.[39] Dealing in uncertain 'futures', while it offers promises of wealth, has never been a secure business. However, when Colt met him, he was still just solvent and hopeful. He would have appeared a man of substance, a real gentleman, and one moreover who had made his fortune from humble beginnings. Phelps had worked as a storekeeper, just like Colt, before joining the Continental army in 1776. He had fought at the Battle of Lexington. Now he was a land speculator on a grand scale with his partner, Gorham, in the process of surveying land he had purchased, and selling it to settlers.

Here was a gentleman for Colt to emulate. Colt, flattered by Phelps' invitation to join him, offered space to the older gentleman in his own waggon, and set off westwards with eleven others.

Years after the events, Colt vividly describes his journey as through a country that became more and more remote:

> we drove our waggon to the Genesee Flats and the road being rough our waggon broak and left it and proceeded from there on horseback, every one carrying his own baggage we proceeded up the Mohawk River through a scattering dutch Settlement, neither the country nor the manner of the people any way inviting & the accommodations very poor. (*Narrative*)

Past Fort Schyler, where Utica is now situated,

> ... at which time there was but one or two log houses... [followed] from a bridle path ... at night encamped on the Canesaraga Flats... On the 12th we reached the Onondaga river and put up at a Major Danford, near the salt springs & the only white Family we found

---

[39] Blaakman, M. (2016).

after leaving Blackmans except a man by the name of Alburt or Talburt who resided in the Castle of Oneida.

This story is one designed to paint a picture of adventure, of travels deeper and deeper into country with no people, no roads, only paths and perilous swamps.

But the clues as to what kind of country he was actually going through are hidden in plain sight. Oneida Castle is named for the Oneida Indians, who were the first residents. It was no French or British 'castle' but one built by the Oneidas themselves, who had successfully defeated the French under Champlain here in 1615. Oneida legend says that the Oneida were led to these lands by following a moving stone; where it stopped, they settled. The name Onyota'a:ka means 'the People of the Standing Stone'. For many years, the Oneida Sacred Stone was in Forest Hill Cemetery in Utica. It was returned to the Oneidas in the 1970s.[40]

Two weeks after leaving Albany, Colt reached the village of Geneva[41] and 'put up at Gilbert R. Beny's'. He had to retrace his steps to retrieve his horse, which had sunk in the mire up to its neck the previous day. On the 17 June he arrived at Canandaigua. In Israel Chapin's cabin he was 'very much fatigued & from the remote situation of the place … and no provision but what was brought in Boats from Albany and Schenecdady there was a … great scarcity of all the necessarys of life.'

Canandaigua is where Colt was to settle. There is some reason to doubt that this is what Colt and his companions 'saw' as they travelled those 17 days westwards, a country he described as ever more wild, ever more distant from the farmlands and villages of Connecticut, with their well-maintained roads, shops, homes, and churches. Certainly the roads were bad, and it seems there was sparse population. But, if we had been with him, what would we have seen along the way?

---

[40] https://oneidacastleny.com/history.php, downloaded 7 July 2020.
[41] Geneva was at the north end of Seneca Lake, and Canandaigua at the head of the adjacent Canandaigua finger lake a few miles to the west.

The fact that, as quoted, he wrote 'the only white Family we found' gives us a clue: he actually did see some families who were not white, but blanked out what he saw. The audience for whom he wrote his *Narrative* were not meant to 'see' them. They were meant to adopt a gaze that saw 'wilderness'. One which saw virgin opportunity. The language he – and his contemporaries – use is often that of an explorer of pristine land. He describes himself as an 'adventurer' who 'took shelter' in a cabin and talks of 'exploring' the land beyond the 'furthermost settlement west of the Mohawk' .

What of other contemporary commentators' descriptions of this 'entire new country'? This part of North America had a violent recent history. Long settled by America's First Nation, in this case the Mohawk, the Seneca and other Iroquois of the Six Nations, this area had been given 'in perpetuity' to them by the British. It lay behind the 1763 Line of Proclamation but had become a battlefield between the British and the Patriots in 1779. The Patriots were ostensibly taking revenge on the British (and their Indian allies) for their attack at Cherry Valley, New York, but with hindsight this 'revenge' seems to have given the republicans an invaluable opportunity to pillage the settled countryside of the Native American nations – to uproot them in readiness for new settlement following any peace with the British (this arrived in 1783, in the Treaty signed in Paris). Patriot militia, approaching from both the Susquehanna and the Mohawk rivers, systematically laid waste to the countryside in 1779. Village after village was destroyed. Although it didn't carry the war all the way to Niagara, as Washington had hoped, the Sullivan-Clinton Campaign as it became known did fulfil both the letter and the spirit of his orders.

'The army had brought a whirlwind of destruction,' according to historian Joseph R. Fischer. 'Their torches had reduced 40 Iroquois towns and villages to ashes and destroyed 160,000 bushels of corn.' Sullivan reported to Washington and Congress there was 'not a single village left in the country of the five nations.' By burning the Iroquois' homes, crops and food stores, his army ensured the deaths of thousands by freezing and starvation during what would be the coldest winter on record at the time. Iroquois men, women and children went begging for shelter at British forts, only to find that their allies had little room and even less compassion for them. Washington did thus succeed in making the Iroquois a burden to and problem for the British.[42]

All this happened just ten years before Colt arrived on the scene. But evidence of the First Nation presence survived. Here is the account of another diarist writing five years after Colt's recounted journey, *The Journal of James Emlen Kept on a Trip to Canandaigua*:

> 23rd. September 1794. We proceeded along the fertile banks of the Tyoga about 16 Miles to the painted Post; in this Morning's travel we crossed many of the Indian's ancient corn fields, the hills in which the Corn was planted being still visible.
>
> ... in passing thro' the Indian Camp some of them were engaged in what they call a War Brag dance, at which time any of spectators have a right, after presenting a Bottle of Rum to make their Boast of what great feats they had done in the course of their Lives. [T]his was done in rotation by the Bystanders, both Indians & Whites, when each in his turn recounted all the heroic Actions of his Life, how many battles he had been in, how many Scalps he had made, how many prisoners he had taken & c. Amongst the rest of the Spectators there being a sensible Doctor of the Neighbourhood present, he after delivering his Bottle, made his Brag,

---

[42] Ron Soodalter, 'Massacre and retribution: The 1779–80 Sullivan Expedition', on Historynet, https://www.historynet.com/massacre-retribution-the-1779-80-sullivan-expedition.htm, downloaded 13 December 2020; Fischer, J.R. (1997) *A Well-Executed Failure: The Sullivan Campaign Against the Iroquois, July–September 1779*, Columbia: University of South Carolina Press, https://www.historynet.com/massacre-retribution-the-1779-80-sullivan-expedition.htm, downloaded 8 October 2020.

which he did by informing them, 'that he had been a Man of peace all his Days, that his profession was to use his utmost endeavours to save Men's Lives, wherein in many instances he hoped that he had been successful, that a Child was capable of taking the Life of a fellow Creature, but that it required a Man of Judgment & Skill to save it.' [T]his kind of boasting being its nature, novel amongst the Indians, gained their universal applause. [43]

Emlen goes on to reflect:

The inhumanity exercised by General Sullivan's Army in cutting down all the Indian Orchards is a subject of Great Regret with the [white] settlers in this Country, no apples being here to be seen, in the late war not only their numerous orchards were destroyed, but 32 of their Towns demolish'd, which drew from the Cornplanter that expressive sentence in his Speech to the President 'When Our Nation call you the Town-destroyer, when our Women hear your Name their faces turn pale & Children cling to the Necks of the Mothers.'[44]

Although some may have thrown themselves on the mercy of the British – there are accounts of refugee camps at Niagara at this period – it is likely that many stayed close to their destroyed villages, and re-inhabited some of them, despite the ensuing hardship and famine. There were certainly many hundreds that arrived before any meeting with the would-be settlers and speculators, or with Federal or State agents in the 1780s and 90s. Colt tells us that upwards of 1,700 camped for two weeks around the village in Canandaigua in the late summer of 1789. This was very soon after his own arrival. He describes them as a curiosity, something alien, and other – 'tribes of Indians', to 'have counsel with' and 'serve with rations'. Images of the merciful (strong),

[43] William N. Fenton (1965), 'The Journal of James Emlen Kept on a Trip to Canandaigua, New York', *Ethnohistory*, 12 (4) (Autumn), pp. 279–342. The journal was written in 1794, so a little later than Colt was in the area, though earlier than his *Narrative* was constructed.

[44] Ibid., p. 317.

Christian distributing alms to the weak. Colt describes a chance meeting with Indians earlier the same summer:

> On a Tour to the Geneseo River, Big Tree Town then called – put up at night near the Honeoy Lake, fell in company with a party of Indians, held a short counsel with them & gave them some provision & Liquor, for which they appeared very Thankful.

Colt was so newly arrived from the East that it is most likely that what he saw (and therefore how he described it) derived from the prejudices, the racism, of the country of his upbringing.

A book of people's memories of the early days, published in 1851,[45] throws another light on the situation. The author, Orsamus Turner, argues, with the benefit of hindsight, that the Native Americans had reason to be discontented with these new white settlers, and a right to demand goods from them. Native Americans had been secure behind the Proclamation Line before 1783; in fact they still contested their right to land to the east of it. They had not been given the money promised by Phelps in the treaty he had made with them on his trip west the year before. (Once Phelps and Gorham had bought the land from New York State, they then had to deal with the 'sitting tenants'.) They had had to 'buy' the land from the people who lived there, in exchange for a small sum, which they had received, plus a yearly annuity, which they hadn't. This whole process more of a 'buying off' than a real transaction. The ancient inhabitants of the area were treated to a bewildering number of 'treaties'. They early dubbed land speculators as 'land jobbers' of whom they were highly suspicious. With good reason. The Native Americans who Colt describes in 1789 were in town to demand payment in goods or cash for that annuity, which had not yet been paid as promised.

---

[45] Turner, O. (1851) *History of the Pioneer Settlement of Phelps and Gorham's Purchase, and Morris' Reserve*: Allegheny County: Alling.

Native American country

The land which Phelps and Gorham were selling to settlers had been lived in for centuries by Native Americans. The occupants of the region had seen their land and villages devastated in the unequal campaign of 1779. Ousted, short changed, no longer under the protection of the British, they had good reason to be hostile. For generations they had co-existed with the white traders, changing their way of life at a manageable pace, growing 'white men's' crops, keeping 'white settlers' livestock, learning French and English languages for trade. At the same time, their white neighbours had adopted many of the farming methods and crops of the Iroquois. Both groups respected the importance of the forests and mountains, the habitat of the wild animals on whom they relied. Men like Phelps and Colt rode roughshod over these well-balanced communities of coexistence.

Increasingly in Colt's *Narrative*, and in other American accounts, the Native Americans were described as 'savages' or 'children'. A people whose methods of life would be improved if they would take on white men's ways. Significantly, their social life, the institutions and traditions of civil society, their laws and customs are no longer mentioned, as they had been by trappers and missionaries at earlier times, and by white people who lived with them for a while and then returned to their families – usually saying how well they had been treated. In the flurry of local histories that were published six decades after the white invasion and takeover, most accounts still term the First Nation 'savages'. Interestingly, Orsamus Turner says he expanded his history of the area to cover the time before Phelps and Gorham arrived – back into the society of Seneca peoples that preceded it. After the 'Excellent Portraits of distinguished Pioneers' (p. vii), he says

> Having adopted the title *Pioneer History of the Holland Purchase*, early events, the first glimpses that our own race had of this region, was indicated as the starting point; and taking position

there, the necessity of going even still farther back, seemed involved. The ancient remains, the mysterious, rude fortifications upon the bluffs, ridges, and banks of streams, throughout our local region, form an interesting feature, and one that claimed a place in our local annals. Some account of our immediate predecessors, the Seneca Iroquois, was suggested as coming within the immediate range of local history; and especially as they were to be mingled in almost our entire narrative. All that relates to them possesses a peculiar interest; that which relates to the system of government of the confederacy to which they belong, is a branch of their history but recently investigated to any considerable extent; is far less generally understood than most things appertaining to them, and has therefore been made to occupy a prominent position in that portion of the work. [Footnote:] The credit of a thorough investigation of this admirable specimen of Indian legislation of unschooled forest statesmanship – and wisdom, if we regard its practical workings – belongs to Lewis H. Morgan, Esq. of Rochester, who communicated the result of his labors, in numbers, to the *North American Review*. In reading his essays, it is difficult to determine which most to admire, the careful and industrious researches of the author, in a matter so difficult to comprehend, with no records, and little beyond obscure tradition for his guides; or the zealous and lively feelings he manifests, in every thing that concerns the character and welfare of the unfortunate race whose interesting traditions he has aided in rescuing from oblivion.[46]

It was now, in 1850, safe to call them an 'unfortunate race'. Their life had been confined to 'reservations' for two generations. But, as occurs throughout the earlier Pioneer narrative, a mixture of racist and derogatory language about the original inhabitants, and a determined effort in this narrative to

[46] Turner, O. (1850) *Pioneer History of the Holland Purchase of Western New York*, Buffalo: Jewett Thomas, p. vi including footnote. The Holland Purchase was part of the Genesee country that Phelps and Gorham sold on to the Holland Land Company.

ignore their presence, distorted reality in favour of the white conquerors. When further peppered with stories of terror and scalpings, these accounts firmly kept the rightful inhabitants of the land at bay.

Chapter 5

The rapid progress of white Anglo-American society in Ontario County

When Colt reached Canandaigua in June 1789, it was hardly more than a plan on paper, with a few marked trees to signify plots, and one or two wooden dwellings – log cabins, rudimentary frame buildings. With, inevitably at that time, the indications of the Native American town so recently destroyed – devastated orchards and fields. The eleven others he had travelled with were only the third group of aspiring settlers to arrive at this spot. The first had arrived the in spring of the previous year. Phelps had spent the winter in Massachusetts and Connecticut encouraging the adventurous to purchase land from him and Gorham. They chose Canandaigua to be the focus of his enterprise, according to Turner, because it was the subject of least conflicting claims from purchasers and State governments at the time. As we saw in the last chapter, this area had been 'sold' by Massachusetts to New York State and then to the private land companies, one of them belonging to Phelps and Gorham.

Settler John Jones wrote of what he saw two months after Colt's arrival. It is startling to read that there hadn't been 'a solitary person there' in 1788, when the area was definitely inhabited by the Native Americans. But like the other settlers, Jones rendered non-white people invisible.

There was a great change. When we left in the fall of '88 there was not a solitary person there; when I returned fourteen months afterwards the place was full of people:– residents, surveyors, explorers, adventurers: houses were going up; it was a busy, thriving place.[47]

---

[47] Turner, O. (1851), p. 165.

Israel Chapin (junior), another New Englander, was in the settlement acting for Phelps and Gorham. He had arrived only a month earlier than Colt, with eight or nine others, and had immediately built himself a log cabin.[48] Colt took lodgings, first with Chapin, then with Oliver Phelps, and was hired on 22 June 'to survey a Township of Land' for Phelps '& a Mr Dennis from Nineveh'.

This was the first of many surveying contracts with Oliver Phelps in 1789. We know that Colt was paid on 30 October for his work. A record exists.

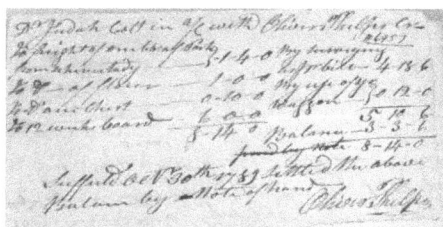

Judah Colt in a/c with Oliver Phelps [archive number] #6957

Dt		Ct	
To Freight of barrel of pork from Schenectady	1-4-0	My surveying as per bill	4-18-6
To d[itto] of flour	1-0-0	My use of your waggon	0-12-0
To d[itto] chest	0-10-0		5-10-6
To 12 weeks board	6-0-0	Balance	3-3-6
	8-14-0		8-14-0

Suffield Oct 30th 1789 settled the above balance by note of hand [signed] Oliver Phelps

Figure 14: Oliver Phelps's record of a payment to Judah Colt for surveying work and attendant costs, Suffield, Connecticut, 30 October 1789.

---

48 Ibid., pp. 163–4.

On 2 July, a fortnight after his arrival, Colt bought a town lot for himself,

> known by No 4 west of Main St, and I same day began to clear & girdle the Timber, on which I afterwards built a dwelling house & resided thereon for several years.

He spent his leisure time in 1789 on his town lot, clearing the land, and sowing on the 10 September 'about 3 acres of wheat on my Town Lot, the first wheat that was ever sowed in this part of the country'.

However, his paid work in these early frontier days was as a surveyor. That Colt was confident of his surveying skills is revealed in his unpublished surveying booklets *Elements of Geometry: Laying of Land and Dividing Land* (March-April 1788, before Colt's final move west) and *Geometrical Problems* (22 January 1830).[49] Both were hand-written, and are faded. Quite how they were used is unclear – he may have taught others who later carried out surveys for the Pennsylvania Population Company, he may have meant to publish them, with his autobiography; but their very existence shows that 'measuring land' was an essential skill, one which Colt was proud of.

Or, did he pay for training? Were these in fact his notes? Was he self taught? We have to assume this was such a new trade that a person (such as Colt) proficient to grammar school level in arithmetic, trigonometry and geometry could take it up fairly easily. No heavy outlay was required to be a surveyor. Andro Linklater describes the westward journey of the first official Geographer of the United States, Thomas Hutchins, in 1785, his team 'armed with two essential instruments, a magnetic compass and twenty two yards of metal links known as Gunter's chain.... Hutchins had axemen to blaze the furthermost tree and hew a track through the undergrowth.'[50]

---

[49] See Bibliography.

[50] Linklater, A. (2015), p. 215.

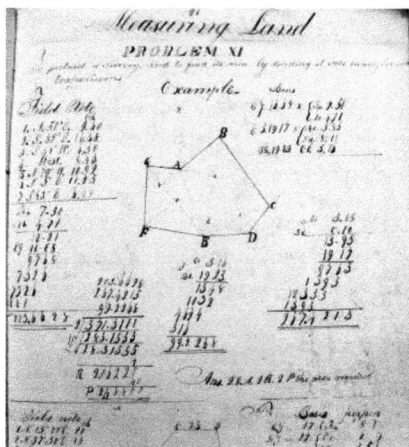

Figure 15: A page from Colt's primer on measuring land, Elements of Geometry: Laying of Land and Dividing Land (1788).

If it appears that the method of surveying described was somewhat rough and ready, it was. Many mistakes were made. Boundaries of lots and of townships were drawn and redrawn over the next 20 years. This imperfection was to be a key irritant in the laying out of civic society on the frontier; and a key income generator for a whole new cohort of lawyers in the United States, using what was essentially still the British legal framework to interpret the hastily drawn Federal and State laws governing land. But in a period when land was prime capital, the measuring kit and attendant skills were well respected.

Colt's first long summer in the West didn't pass without mishap. Phelps remarks with concern that the majority of his settlers went down with 'the ague' – which we now know was malaria. With no doctor to call at that time, sufferers had to sweat it out. Phelps was clear to Colt he caught it 'through wading through Streams & Swamps'. For the speculators trying to make a profit from their bulk purchases of huge tracts of land, this was a big issue. Although not many deaths were recorded from the ague in the area at this time, it was a worry in all the new settlements, as the respondents told Orsamus Turner in the 1850s. With so many incapacitated from the fever, and no obvious cure, this ague was bound to put off purchasers and slow down settlements.

A rare appearance of Native Americans in Colt's *Narrative*

As we've seen, there are few Native Americans in Colt's *Narrative*. They do however play a part as a set piece description in 1789. They appear as a vast group of 'about 1700 Indians of men women & children that were served with rations of Bread & Meat and occasionally Rum'. They remained 'encamped about a Mile out of Town' – Canandaigua, by then designated the County Town of Ontario County, New York – from 27 July to 6 of August. 'Several Tribes of Indians were coming in to Treat with him [Mr Phelps] for the purchase of their land . (In fact, as recounted above, the treaty itself took place the previous year. As recounted by Turner (1851), the 'several tribes' had accepted Phelps and Gorham's offer of $10,000 (itself a cheatingly meagre amount) for their land, together with a $500 annuity. At this new encounter, the 'several tribes' were claiming the $5,000 that they had yet to receive, as well as the promised yearly annuity.) The word 'tribes' immediately summons an image of some more primitive state of mankind than the white villagers. They also had quaint ways – 'The Chiefs were seated on a large circul on the Ground, who, when we arrived, arose, took us by the hand and led us to the centre, where we sat down.' Phelps invited them in to the village, 'when the Chiefs preceded the Womin and displayed sundry Indian Military Manoevers after which they were treated with Rum and Provisions and the day ended pleasantly'. The language is carefully chosen – 'military manoeuvres' suggests they were war-like, 'treated' suggests the white villagers were being generous, charitable, to people in need. The description goes on to suggest this was an expensive undertaking (great generosity) – 'upwards of 100 heads of cattle was killed for them', and uncouth: 'many horses died distempered during the Treaty, the Indians fed on them freely & also the blood & entrails of all the Beef slautered.'

> Although no serious accidents happened between the Whites & Indians there was several narrow escapes in consequence of the Indians making too free use of Spirits – and the Misconduct of the white people who were often the aggressors. (*Narrative*)

Colt's hindsight includes some subtlety: A suspicion of danger is conjured up (too free use of spirits), but at the same time he is prepared to stand up for the 'Indian' (white people were the aggressors). But overall, he manages to leave an impression that Phelps was in the right, bending over backwards to accommodate, generously provisioning these 1,700 people for over a week.

Given the double-dealing of the land dealers, it is staggering that the First Nation community didn't simply overwhelm the eight households in the newly laid out village that was already obliterating the fair fields and orchards of those original Seneca inhabitants.

Colt travels back to Connecticut for the winter

Colt's ague came and went, but by 3 of October in that, his first, year in Upper New York State,

> when despairing of getting rid of the Ague, I concluded to leave the Country, ... accordingly on the 4th of October I set out in a Battoe in company with Moses Atwater and sundry others ... on the 14th I arrived at the Town of Lansingburgh & put up with my friend Charles Selden[51] and by changing my diet and taking plentifully of the bark, I got rid of the ague, but was taken with influenza which continued with me very severely until 22nd, when feeling on the mending hand, set out for Connecticut. (*Narrative*)

I discuss medicine later on, but it is worth saying here that 'the ague' nearly did for those first settlers. Each of the new

---

[51] Possibly a relative of the Thomas Shelden mentioned earlier, or else a mistake on Colt's part.

settlements was laid low, pretty well incapacitated at times, by the malarial fever. It didn't seem to kill people, just left them with a chronic sickness. And Canandaigua, like many settlements, didn't have a doctor. The fact that Colt felt he had to go back east for a cure – where he took 'plentifully of the bark' – i.e. quinine also known as Peruvian bark in the eighteenth century – suggests he hadn't found a cure on the frontier. The acute problem with malaria seems to have cleared up fairly soon, though the mosquitoes were still around. Did the new white settlers turn to their Native American neighbours for cures and simply not record this? Did the doctors? Or, as the land was cleared and farmed New England fashion, and the houses made more substantial, was the risk of infection diminished?

On his way home, Colt stocked up with land so he could sell to the good people of Connecticut – presumably either as investment – that they could sell on to others – or to settle themselves. From his *Narrative*:

> Travelled through Williamstown in Massachusetts, Pittsfield, and from thence to Granville [N.Y.], called on a Mr. Ebenezer Curtis of whom I had purchased a lot of land, containing 640 acres and received of him a deed – a Tract of Land which I sold afterward to ... Henry Chauncey & Richard McCurdy. From Granville road to Suffield [Conn.], settled accounts with Oliver Phelps & purchased of him & received a deed for a Lot of Land...

640 acres is enough for a small village. He had reason to be pleased. He carefully records these purchases – and the deeds – so there was no doubt these were bought up front, not on credit. But we know that these deeds still had to be translated into something 'run off' – surveyed. Here is the very heart of land 'speculation' from the period. And he is pursuing his other linked enterprises:

> ... & from thence, shaped my course for Lichfield, for the purpose of seeing & settling some business with Thomas Shelden.

This looks like an opportunity to buy and sell dry goods from the merchant he had worked for as a bookkeeper back in 1788. Finally he arrived home.

I have experienced much hardship & Sickness I considered the Tour a very fortunate one and laid the foundation of an increasing fortune.

Colt's vision of future wealth and land – the life of a gentleman – was on the way to fruition.

Colt's second year in the Genesee country

Colt set off by himself the following spring, 1790, to take up the new settlement anew. On the way he fell in with the Sanborn family – Hannah Sanborn originally came from Lyme. They hired a batteau together for their goods, and set off up the Mohawk. This was a transport method far superior to that of the previous year, a horse and cart; Colt could now afford more comfort. When she was 88 years old, Hannah Sanborn related her memory of the journey to Orsamus Turner. She explained that Utica was the 'last house she slept in' on the way west before arriving in Canandaigua – and that they 'camped wherever night overtook them'; that 'on the Oswego River they took possession of a deserted camp and that, just as they had got their supper prepared, two stout Indians came who claimed the camp and threatened a summary ejectment. The conflicting claim was amicably adjusted.' But Mrs Sanborn goes on to say, 'this was the first of the race she had ever seen and they cost her a little fright. The party saw none but Indians and boatmen in all the long journey west of Utica.'[52]

Colt himself records the journey quite differently. On his way back west, after having several more bouts of the fever – he records as 'influenza' – over the winter, in April he travelled to Albany on horseback:

---

[52] Turner, O. (1851), pp. 165–6.

... and from thence to Schenectady, where I met Nathaniel Sandbarn [Sanborn] & Family and between us we purchased a Battoe, on board which he put his family and our effects of Provisions &c, &c, and 1st May of a Saturday we set off with our Battoe for Schenectady up the Mohawk River & through the chain of waters to the Outlet of the Canadaqua [Canandaigua] Lake and after a passage of 28 days of hard labour we arrived safe at Phelps Landing, so called, about seven miles from Canadaqua. (Narrative)

RIVER SCENE SHOWING FLATBOAT AND TWO KEELBOATS

Figure 16: A batteau, or battoe, and keelboats.[53]

No mention of the deserted camp or the stout Indians of Hannah's account. No mention of Hannah, or the rest of the Sanborn family. All invisible. The only thing Colt considered worth registering was his and Nathaniel's hard labour. Both of these accounts are from memory, Hannah Sanborn's written in 1850, Colt's probably in 1808.

Hannah Sanborn, then, did notice the Native Americans. However they 'cost her a little fright'. And she names a village a

---

[53] Source: Buck, S. and E. (1949), p. 249.

'camp'. And talks about 'conflicting claims' when the Native Americans would have been quite clear in whose village the Sanborn/Colt party were spending the night. Mrs Sanborn gives another description of the 'Indians', four years later, when she and her husband were well established as the main innkeepers in the growing town of Canandaigua. In both descriptions, Mrs Sanborn reveals her view of these people as 'other', frightening – she says they were 'the first of the race she had ever seen' – despite her upbringing in Lyme which will have brought her into contact with many dispossessed Native American families. She describes them 'creating a sensation of novelty, not unmingled with fear', and 'the little village of whites overrun with the wild natives'.[54] The words used in her recollections tell us of the war of words being waged by the settlers: 'first of the race', 'novelty', 'fear', 'overrun', 'wild natives'.

Colt's fellow surveyor Augustus Porter (see next chapter) arrived aged 20 in Bloomfield just west of Canandaigua in the summer of 1789. According to Orsamus Turner:

> When he arrived he found the Adams family, and those who had come in with them, the occupants of a log house 30 by 40 feet, the first dwelling erected west of Canandaigua after white settlement commenced. To accommodate so large a family with lodgings, there were berths upon wooden pins along the walls of the house, one above the other, steam, or packet boat fashion. It was the young surveyor's first introduction to backwoods life. He added to the crowded household himself and his assistants, and soon shouldered his 'Jacob's staff', and commenced his work. The emigrants had brought on a good stock of provisions and some cows: wild game soon began to be added, which made them very comfortable livers. The Judge, in his later years, would speak with much animation, of the primitive log house, its enormous fireplace; and especially the bread 'baked in ashes' which Mrs Rose used to bring upon the table, and which he said was excellent.[55]

---

[54] Turner. O. (1851), p. 187.

[55] Ibid., p. 188.

In 1790, Porter assisted John Fellows, a Massachusetts war hero (Brigadier General), sheriff and State representative who had been allotted 3,000 acres by the Army and owned other land in the area. The same year Fellows and Porter erected the sawmill on Mud Creek, near Canandaigua – a sure line of profit. Although Porter stayed in the West, Fellows went home to Massachusetts, much discouraged, and sold his lands at 18 pence an acre, thinking that even if the wheat was good, finding a market was too difficult.[56] This was a fast-moving situation – people coming and going, making and losing money in ventures, while the settlements grew and the infrastructure bedded in.

Orsamus Turner's and Henry O'Reilly's histories

Two histories of Ontario County were written in the mid-nineteenth century. Orsamus Turner's whole enterprise was to make and sell an account that was as vivid as possible. *The History of the Pioneer Settlement of Phelps and Gorham Purchase and Morris's Reserve*, published in 1851, came after the success of his *History of the Holland Purchase* published 1850 and a book by O'Reilly on the settlement of the area 12 years before.[57] Both writers were journalists in the town of Buffalo, by mid-century a thriving industrial town benefitting from the Erie Canal lank between the Hudson River and the Great Lakes. All three books sold well. They elevated the early settlers into 'early pioneers'– at a time when families were pouring much further west to settle the vast plains and far mountains of the United States. The story of pioneering that had taken place in their own communities, so recently, clearly struck a chord with their readers in the towns and settled rural farmlands of New York State. The original inhabitants, who are firmly depicted as savages – and beggars – were consigned to a bit-part in the history of a second creation on 'Canaan's land', as Turner styled the area. This was above all

---

[56] Turner, O. (1850), p. 174.

[57] O'Reilly, H. (1838), *Sketches of Rochester*, Rochester: William Alling.

a eulogy to the 'pioneer' settlers. And the right kind of settler, in Turner's view, were New Englanders. Like Colt.

As mentioned, Turner tells the pre-history of the region – when the Native Americans and the trappers lived in mutual respect and harmony. Because, from the safety of 80 years of white settlement, which had seen the destruction of the forests and an entire way of life – and the relegation of Native Americans to the margins of the new society, in reservations, selling dolls, fish, baskets, just as they did in New England – it was finally possible for white historians to tell the story of an earlier civilisation that might have had some good points. Turner swiftly narrates his version of the Revolution, and the Sullivan-Clinton onslaught on the British Native Americans in New York State – from Canajoharie to Fort Niagara. He follows this up with stories of the 'Indian' treaties, where Federal government spokesmen, State officials, and land speculators take turns in parleying with people styled as 'savages', 'starving supplicants', 'children', 'squaws' and 'sachems', members of 'tribes' – anything to reduce them to some kind of non-people. After giving his readers the idea that justice had been done, he introduces the old settlers he has interviewed who were there from the beginning (the late 1780s).

Drawing on letters and other written material, Turner builds a picture of the rapid construction of white, New Englander-dominated civil society in this uncharted territory which closely chimes with Colt's account. Seamlessly he shifts focus from a country supporting a well-ordered economy of First Nation villages and white traders, 'your immediate predecessors, the Seneca Iroquois', to one built from scratch in a 'wilderness' needing to be tamed. In his dedication (to the early pioneers, of course) he writes:

> ... you live to be the witness of more than it is often given man to see. The wilderness you entered in your youths – some of you in middle age – you have lived to see not only 'blossom as the rose'

but to bear its mature and ripened fruit ... you began to wield the axe in the forests of the Genesee country.... A subtle agent ... flashing in the dark forests, indicating its power by scathing and levelling its tall trees; then but partially subdued to man's use; now tamed, harnessed, controlled ... breaking out from their quiet New England homes, in youth and strength, went first to battlefield ... then after a short respite came to this primitive region, and won a local inheritance for you, fair and fertile... [58]

Turner returns to this theme after rehearsing the early history of the region:

To eyes that had rested only upon the rugged scenery of New England, its mountains and rocky hill sides, its sterile soil and stinted herbage, the march must have afforded a constant succession of beautiful landscapes; and what was of greater interest to them, practical working men as they were, was the rich easily cultivated soil, that at every step caused them to look forward to the period when they could make to it a second advent – a peaceful one – with the implements of agriculture, rather than the weapons of war.... Returning to the firesides of Eastern New York, and New England, they relived the dark picture of retaliatory warfare ... the flight, the smouldering cabins, pillage and spoliation – with the lighter shades – descriptions of the Lakes and Rivers, the rolling uplands and rich valleys – the Canaan of the wilderness, they had seen.[59]

In Turner's version of history, the only 'war' was the Sullivan-Clinton expedition of 1779. He recounts the subsequent treaties designed to buy off the Native American inhabitants, and the settlers' relentless annexation of land and forest, and continuing rout and dispossession of a whole people. In his account, these treaties, with the annuities and handouts, and confirmation of 'reservation land', become something generous, that the settlers

---

[58] Turner. O. (1851), pp. iii, iv.

[59] Turner, O. (1851), p. 130.

were bestowing on the First Nation. The land was by then in State and private hands – ripe for improvement. He uses Christian Biblical imagery – 'advent', 'Canaan of the wilderness' – and talks of the peace and prosperity brought to the region by the settlers. He allows that the treaties sometimes might not have been just – but this was a matter of amount. When Phelps and Gorham had 'bought' the goodwill of the First Nation, they had agreed to give them an annuity – every year in perpetuity – for their land. Whether this was to acknowledge it was leasehold, or whether as a sweetener to make them go away, or whether it was because the main sum wasn't enough even in the eyes of Phelps and Gorham so the annuity was to top up the amount, the treaties are not clear enough to say categorically one way or the other. In any case, the annuity agreed by Phelps and Gorham ceased to be paid within a decade. As far as Turner is concerned the land was now in the hands of people who harnessed it to produce riches – much better hands than the previous owners of the earth.

The triumphant tone of the mid-nineteenth century was expressed in a New England journal:

> The Wild forests are cleared away, the green slopes are dressed and laid out smiling at the sun, the hills and valleys are adorned with beautiful structures, the skin of wild beasts are laid aside for robes of silk or wool. In a word, architecture, gardening, music, dress, chaste and elegant manners – all inventions of human taste – are added to the rudimentary beauty of the world, and it shines forth, as having undergone a second creation at the hand of man.[60]

So, language is used to obliterate what had been a brutal dispossession. A dispossession all the easier to accomplish by New Englanders who lived in similarly conquered land – that their forebears had expropriated for themselves, while the conquered continued marginalised and, although in plain sight, rendered comfortingly invisible. The scene was set for

---

[60] 'Taste and fashion', *New Englander and Yale Review* 1 (1843), quoted in Nye, D. (2003), epigraph.

settlement. Turner, the chronicler, tells us that pre-1776, apart from a very few white families, an Indian interpreter and a few traders, 'All else was Seneca Indian occupancy'.[61] And he quotes General Micah Brooks, whose retentive memory goes back to the period. Brooks remembers soldiers discharged without pay, scanty crops, a country reduced to poverty and commerce nearly annihilated, fisheries abandoned and a huge national debt. He remembers a new sort of young labourer who had been in Sullivan-Clinton's armies who wished to

> chastise the savages for cruelties inflicted on their friends and relations ... with their families, under the guidance and protection of a kind Providence [note God conveniently on their side] ... pioneered the way through a long wilderness, to the land of promise – the Genesee country.[62]

Turner allows Brooks' testimony to show the rapid success and format of the settlements: 'In seven or eight years from the first entrance of a settler, a number of towns in Ontario County were furnished with well chosen public libraries.' Brooks – and Turner – see libraries as the mark of a town that has properly arrived and with it, civilisation.

Early years in Canandaigua

Canandaigua, Colt's first western home, we learn from Turner's book, was surveyed during 1788 and 1789. It was laid out in farm lots, along a main street at right angles to the lake of Canandaigua. Phelps first erected a store house, and then laid 'primitive roads ... following pretty much the old Indian trail.' No-one stayed overwinter in 1788.

In the spring of 1789 Joseph Smith moved from Geneva to the store house. He soon built a block house and opened a tavern. These two buildings welcomed the trickle of new settlers who

---

[61] Turner, O. (1851), p. 128.

[62] Turner, O. (1851), p. 134.

arrived in May and June, including Colt. General Israel Chapin built the first log house, where Colt briefly lodged. Soon after, others arrived including a Mr Walker, agent of Phelps and Gorham, who opened a land office, where Colt was hired. Jones, one of the early settlers, recalled:

> There was a great change. When we left in the Fall of '88 there was not a solitary person there; when I returned fourteen months afterwards the place was full of people:- residents, surveyors, explorers, adventurers; houses were going up; it was a busy, thriving place.[63]

According to Turner, Canandaigua was the 'centre of the Indian trade' from its white settler beginning in 1788, and the place Native Americans came to for their annuities.

The first religious meetings were held in 1790, in Judge Phelps's new barn. The town meeting convened for the first time in 1791. Mrs Sanborn remembered 'friendship, good feeling, hilarity, athletic games, were the order of the day.'[64] The business of the meeting? To agree a bounty of 30 shillings on any wolf killed and to demand pigs should be yoked.[65]

The two maps, 'Country of the VI Nations' (1771) and 'Messers Gorham and Phelps's Purchase: Now the County of Ontario in the State of New York' (1794), show graphically how the country was imagined before and after the 1783 Treaty of Paris. By the 1790s, Colt's time, the map comprised a set of rectangles, ripe for development. The surveyors had the unenviable task of taking the maps of these forests and swamps – maps isn't a good description – paper with ruled lines and numbers on it better – that represented the huge tract Oliver Phelps and Stephen Gorham had bought, simply ruled out in squares or rectangles in an office back east. They took these paper plans with their

---

[63] Turner, O. (1851), p. 165.

[64] Turner, O. (1851), p. 169.

[65] Ibid., p. 172.

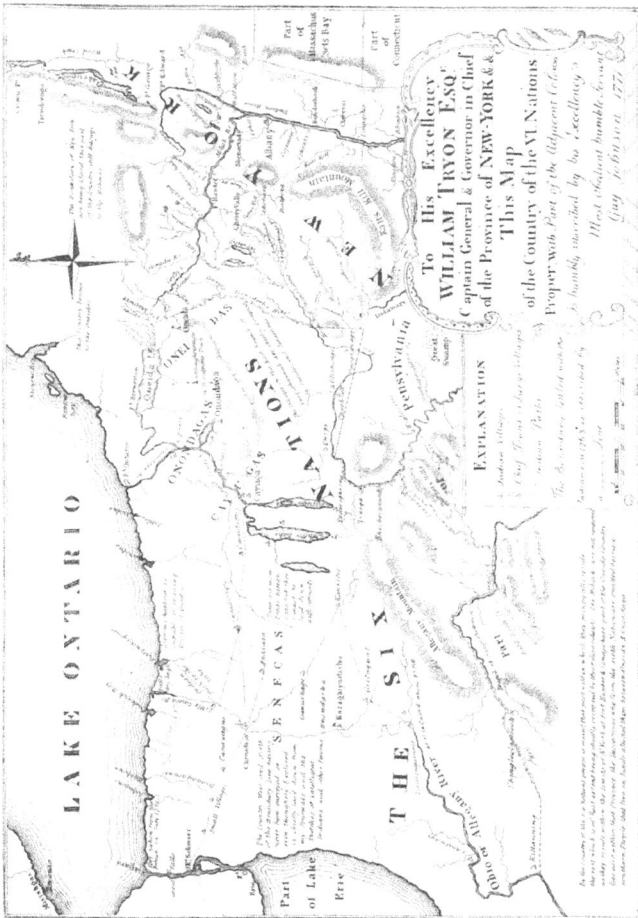

Figures 17 and 18 (above and overleaf): Before and after the dispossession: 'The Land of the Iroquois' (1771), showing Native American villages and townships; and 'Messers Gorham and Phelps's Purchase: Now the County of Ontario in the State of New York' (1794), showing the carve-up and erasure.[66]

Jacob's staffs and chains, and scarred the trees in the corners of
the vast plots in readiness for a settler to come and buy it – on
credit, usually – and start to clear it and put up house and barns.
In the 1790 Federal Census, the plot or village in Ontario County
was described with its township and range numbers.

Canandaigua was described in the Gorham and Phelps Purchase as 'T10 R3' (10th township in the 3rd range: see map). Ten years later, the settlements were known by name only, not 'T', 'R' any more. This was rapid permanent settlement indeed.

There were problems which had to be overcome. Disease was prevalent in those first years. The indigenous people had many herbal remedies, and traditional sweating cures. But the new settlers wanted their own white medicine. Until 1791, the population, which was laid low with chronic diseases we now know as malaria, yellow fever, and dysentery, had to rely on their own resources – the nearest doctor was in Geneva, at least half a day's ride away, even when the roads were passable. The mosquitoes do appear to have been especially fierce in the Genesee country – here are the words of a British traveller in 1800:

> The mosquitoes of this swampy district were of a stouter race than any I had yet encountered, and to my utter astonishment, I found them capable of drawing blood through a thick leather riding glove.[67]

Dr Coventry reminisces about his practice at nearby Geneva:

> On the 7th of June, 1792 I arrived with my family at my former residence near the outlet of Seneca Lake, opposite to the village of Geneva. The seasons of 1793 and 1794 were very sickly in the Genesee Country in proportion to the population. There was a much greater number of cases of fever than in the cities, although they were not so fatal in their termination. I remember a time when, in the village of Geneva, there was but a single individual who could leave her bed, and for several days she alone, like a ministering angel, went from house to house, bestowing on the sick the greatest of all boons – a drink of cold water. During the season mentioned, dysenteries occasionally appeared, preceding or following, and sometimes alternating with the fever. In 1795 no rain fell either in June or July – the waters in the lakes lowered

---

[67] Quoted in Turner, O. (1850), p. 152.

more than a foot – every little inlet became a seat of putrefaction – the heavens seemed on fire, the earth scorched, and the air saturated with pestilence – the hogs were found dead in the woods, the flies swelled and turned white, and lay in handfuls on the floors of our rooms. On the 18th of August I was called to visit Judge P. at Aurora, on the east side of the Cayuga, whose house, I believe, was the first one that had been built on the Military Tract: one apartment contained the corpse of his wife, who had expired a few hours before my arrival, with every symptom attendant on malignant or yellow fever; in another apartment the judge and two children lay with very threatening symptoms. While attending here on the night of the 22nd, I heard the pleasant sound of thunder, and soon after the more delightful noise of the rain pattering on the roof, with which our ears had not been regaled for the last two months. A change of at least twenty degrees of temperature followed, together with a copious fall of water. The patients labouring under fever seemed to be immediately benefited, and the new cases decreased. But dysentery soon made its appearance in the most appalling and fatal form – occasioned, without doubt, by this sudden change of temperature, causing a checked perspiration in persons fully prepared. On my return I found that three persons had died of dysentery on the preceding day in the village of Geneva, and was informed that several others lay at the point of death.[68]

The first physician to live in Canandaigua itself was Dr Moses Atwater, who arrived in 1791 (Atwater was born in Connecticut).[69] He seems to have purchased a house there

---

[68] Williams, S.W. (1845) *American Medical Biography or Memoirs of Eminent Physicians*, Greenfield, Mass.: Merriam and Co.: 'Dr Coventry: born in Scotland, he emigrated to Hudson to look at some property he'd inherited from his father. In 1785 he married Elizabeth Butler from Branford, Connecticut. He lived in Romulus on Seneca lake until 1796 when on account of the sickness he moved to Fort Schuyler now Utica', (pp. 110–11); O'Reilly, H. (1838), p. 91.

[69] Turner, O. (1851), p. 179.

n advance of his arrival, which Colt lived in (see below).

Almost all the people who settled in Canandaigua in its first years were from Connecticut and Massachusetts. Many were known to each other, had families who intermarried, long before coming west. Some came as whole families – cousins, brothers and sisters.

Canandaigua was well on the way, in only its third season, to being a town that closely resembled the New England towns most of the inhabitants came from.

Colt's own part in the rapid settlement follows the pattern of other settlers – with the exception that he has no backstory as a soldier. He is already using his talents to make his fortune in the diverse ways open to him. Below we follow the continuation of his frontier career from 1790 as he enters his 29th year, his second in Canandaigua:

> I resided in a small log house owned by Moses Atwater & kept Bachelor's Hall. Thomas Lord the son of John Lord was hired with me from June until September – in the fall I erected me a small Log House.

Despite more attacks of fever, he remained busy, surveying townships in the district, building his house and ploughing and planting his farm.

> In the course of the summer I received a commission from his Excellency George Clinton Esqr appointing me Sheriff of Ontario County, and on the 3rd day of September a Court of Quarter Sessions a general Sessions of the Peace [sic] was held at the then dwelling house of Ollipher [Oliver] Phelps, and since owned by Moses Atwater. Oliver Phelps Esqr presided as Judge and James Parker and Israel Capens [Chapin] as assistant Justices. (*Narrative*)

On the recommendation of Phelps, or Chapin, or Gorham – or all three, the Governor of the State of New York[70] had

---

[70] George Clinton, later US Vice President, was a younger brother of James Clinton of the infamous Sullivan-Clinton campaign.

accepted Colt as a key member of the new-minted community. This was confirmation indeed that, educated, energetic, a farmer and a surveyor, Colt was a good candidate to help keep order and maintain the law in the new community. Colt is at pains to tell us that in 1790 the rule of law was established in Canandaigua and the surrounding Ontario County with a full complement of judges, assistants, and himself as Sheriff. All this less than three years from when the first house was built, when there were still only a handful of families.

Colt spent his second summer on the frontier farming and surveying. He extended his acreage – not only ploughing and planting his own plot in Canandaigua, but also buying, clearing, ploughing and seeding others – whether to sell on at a higher price or to keep and rent out we don't know. On his town lot he planted 'Oats, Buckwheat, and Corn, all of which succeeded well'.

On one occasion, coming back from the Geneseo River valley (Big Tree Town) through Township 11 (Honeoye), he

> purchased a yoak of Oxen of Joseph Morgan, price 50 Dollars, which enabled me to prepare & put in crops about 12 acres of wheat. I returned back to Canandaigua on the 8th, and on the 9th of August began to harvest my wheat which I had sowed on the front of my town lot in the fall of 1789 – yielding average of 20 bushels to the acre.

Colt is hammering home the astonishing fertility of this country. And the lesson that hard work could indeed build a fortune. This is the story that chroniclers, more than a generation later, wanted to glorify.

The only hint Colt gave that year that this land had recently had other inhabitants, and that they were still in the area, was that he marked the death of a young man 'the first white man that died in this Village since the first settlement.' Was he admitting in his *Narrative* that there were non-white inhabitants, and but that any non-white deaths were to remain invisible?

That autumn (1790) he built himself a house and hired himself a workman. Both these, and being a Sheriff, helped to earn him the title he began to give himself in documents – 'Esquire'. There is a social hierarchy here already. He is telling us – and himself – that he has climbed the social ladder.

With this in mind, it is worth turning to the 1790 Census, the first in the new United States. Across the country, this Census provides a wonderfully varied set of documents, much dependent on the clerk who compiled them. The Census for Canandaigua, written in the confident hand of Amos Hall, sheds light on the inhabitants. The headings are clear: Name of heads of families / Free white males, 16 years and upwards including heads of families/ Free white males under sixteen years / Free white females including heads of families / All other free persons / Slaves. There are 88 male heads of families. In these 88 households lived 203 more males over 16 years, many of whom must have been hired hands, and 60 males under 16.

Also in these households lived 111 females of all ages. There appear to be no female heads of families. The single 'Other free person' fell in a category used for persons of colour and freed indentured servants. The slaves we can see belong to Israel Chapin Junior (six) and Joseph Smith (one). The photograph, from the Federal Census office, does not allow us to see the 'Slaves' column on the second page.

The majority of the households are of two or three adult males. The biggest are those of Reed (18 people), Potter (14), Reed, and Sanbourne (Sanborn) (11), who ran a tavern, Fellows (11), Chapin (10) and Wilder (11). According to the Findagrave online resource, most of the 88 male 'Heads of Families' who later died in Canandaigua were Massachusetts or Connecticut born. Only three are styled 'Esquire' – Seth Reed, Nathaniel Gorham and Colt himself, all office holders. They were all from New England. The stark fact is that the Census shows an unequal society closely mirroring a New England pattern.

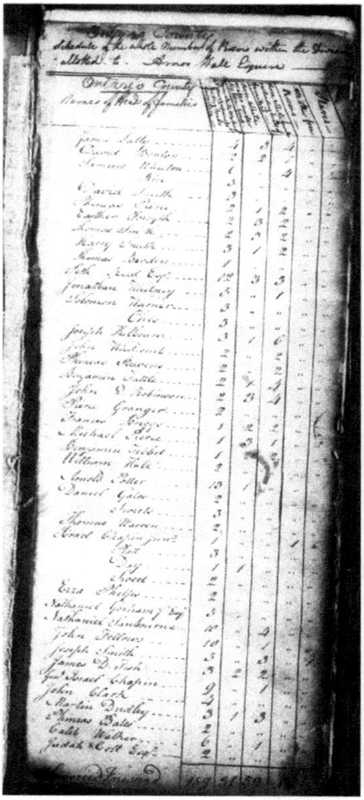

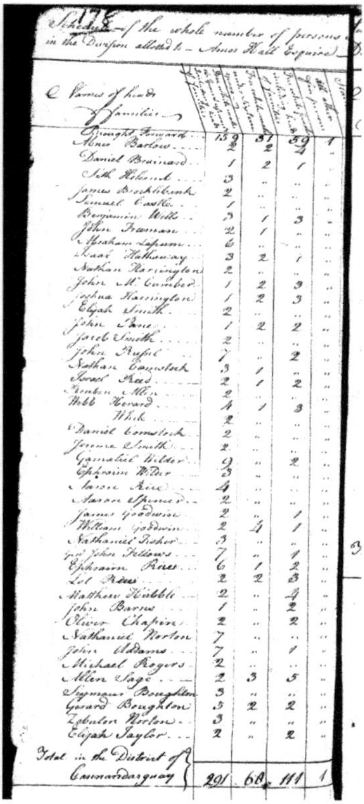

Figures 19 and 20: The Federal Census of 1790: 'Ontario County: Schedule of the whole number of persons in the division allotted to Amos Hall Esquire ... District of Cannandaiguay'. The column headings are: 'Name of heads of families / Free white males, 16 years and upwards including heads of families/ Free white males under sixteen years / Free white females including heads of families / All other free persons / Slaves'.[71]

---

[71] United States Census, 1790, Canandaigua, Ontario County, New York State.

1791–94: Freemasonry, another rung in the ladder

After another winter back home in Lyme, where he 'made some advances towards matrimony', Colt set off again, this time with hired help, Nathan Phelps, son of his boss Oliver Phelps. Narrating this year – 1791 (his 30th) – Colt sees fit to read us a sermon on his safe arrival back in Canandaigua with a new load of provisions:

> Thus we are travelling through life striving to lay up Treasure on Earth to shun the poverty which we dread, a prudent & industrious care, for to provide for ourselves & our household is commendable, but to lay up Treasure for the World to Come, Yea durable riches, is far more to be prized and desired, than any possible earthly enjoyment, and ought to consider ourselves as strangers & pilgrims, travel to a better Country. (*Narrative*)

Colt is, somewhat sanctimoniously, berating himself here for toiling to become wealthy in his lifetime – when he should be living a life of Christian goodness, charity, generosity to others, a life of humility, not pride. He moves back into his new house, and notes the growth of the village.

> The prospect of the country becoming populous is Very flattering, great number of Families moved into the settlement during the winter and Spring, principally from Massachusetts and Connecticut, who bring with them their steady habits – The people generally conveaned on the Sabbath for worship sermons were read and Psalms were sung.

These were not just sober, steady folk, they were steadfast Christians. That summer he built a barn and 'pursued his ordinary business successfully'.

He also must have joined the local band of freemasons, because that winter – 1791 – he was asked to visit the grand master in New York on behalf of the nine gentlemen masons of

Ontario County[72] – Timothy Hosmer, Samuel Mellish, Judah Colt, Otho J. Taylor, John Chapin, Jr., Benjamin Wells, Seth Reed, William Adams and Thomas Morris. We have encountered some of these leading local personages, or will do so. The purpose of the visit was to convey an application to set up a lodge. Being asked to join the brotherhood of masons was a significant step. Freemasons at that time were – and still are in the present – men who embraced the responsibility of helping their fellow men (and women) – and helping each other be responsible, philanthropic human beings, above and beyond their duty as Christians. These 'brotherhoods' were secretive, powerful groups of the elite of a community. By their nature they were groups that entrenched social hierarchy, self-defining as the best even if they were theoretically open to all social classes. Freemasonry was European in origin, championing ideas of enlightenment and liberty. It had spread to the Colonies in the early eighteenth century. Freemasonry remained important after the Revolution in the early Republic. Freemasons are not mentioned by Colt again in his *Narrative* or in his more detailed accounts, but his membership is likely to have continued and to have ensured his social standing. We know from the records of the Ontario chapter to which he belonged that it gave out charitable loans – often to travellers, for aid – over the next few years, to the sum of $250 – all but $50 was written off as a bad debt – securing food and medicine, acting as a charity for the poor white settlers.[73]

That third summer in Canandaigua Colt does mention the Native Americans again – but, as before, only as a set piece description of 'otherness' in their abject poverty, supplication and strange habits.

---

[72] McIntosh, W.H., Hanger, G.M., Pitts, C.P. (1876) *History of Ontario Co., New York: With Illustrations Descriptive of Its Scenery, Palatial Residences, Public Buildings, Fine Blocks, and Important Manufactories*, Philadelphia: Everts, Ensign & Everts, p. 63.

[73] Heinmiller, G.L. (2010) *Craft Masonry in Ontario, Seneca and Yates Counties, New York,* Onondaga and Oswego Masonic District Historical Society.

In the course of this Month, July 1791, a Treaty was held with the Seneca Nations of Indians at New Town, present on the part of the U States, Timothy Pickering Esqr. This Treaty was on account of sundry Indians which had been killed by white People on the waters of the Susquehannah & elsewhere viz Pine Creek – Oliver Phelps Esquire attended this Treaty from this county.[74] (*Narrative*)

Here Colt summons up the authority of the Federal government – merciful and just. Timothy Pickering was George Washington's commissioner to the Iroquois Indians.

In December 1791 he was back in Connecticut. He married Elizabeth Marvin of Lyme, 'by mutual consent'. The banns were published on Christmas Day and they were married on the 8 January. Leaving his wife in Lyme, he went on to New York. First, 'while in the City I spent some time in the House of Assembly where I fell in company with Col. Leuly [Lindsley] our first member of assembly from Ontario County who had lately arrived and taken his seat in the house.' Colt is good at taking advantage of 'making connections'. He then went on to fulfil his mission for the Ontario County Masons.

I was also a bearer of a Petition from the Masons of Ontario for obtaining a Charter for a Lodge from the Grand Lodge in this City & was introduced to Chansellor Livingstone for that purpose, who then presided as Grandmaster, the Petition was granted. (*Narrative*)

Returned to Lyme, he commenced his annual business of selling land and buying equipment, which he lays out in some detail.

... during this time sold sundry lots of land, to Reverend Henry Channing of New London for a small advance which enabled me to purchase a Team of oxen & Span of Horses and Sleigh for the purpose of moving Mrs Colt & Self & our household goods to Geneseo.

[74] This was a prelude to the Canandaigua Treaty of 1794 (see next chapter). See Oberg, M.L (2016) *Peacemakers: The Iroquois, the United States, and the Treaty of Canandaigua, 1794*, Oxford: OUP.

He details the journey – 'good sleighing' and 'arriving in 'good health'. The newly married couple settled into his new house. He spent the summer farming, executing duties of 'My Office of Sheriff' – in 'good health, and quietly settled in life, in a flourishing New Country'. As far as Colt tells us, the main risks were illness and travel – and he had triumphed over those and was now settled.

Visiting preachers were a feature of the period. We hear who 'partook of the sacrament', which was administered 'for the first time in this part of the Country': Isaac Chapin Esq., and wife, the Whitmores, the Wilders, Warner and Pitts – '7 in all'. Divine services, the coming of formal Christianity to the settlement, may have been later in arrival than the taverns (run by the Sanborns and the Smiths) and the law, but they were definitely a sign of bedding in.

So too was the advent of the militia. In November that year,

> Several Companies of Militia assembled this day in town and were inspected and Manoevred under the direction and command of Col. Otherial Taylor. This was the first military parade of the kind since the settlement of the Country. (*Narrative*)

The law, the Masonic lodge, religion and a militia to keep order, a doctor – all the trappings of a well-ordered civil society in the image of an Anglo-American colonial community like that of Lyme. Colt must have been elated. What was being built was a familiar society – one of social hierarchy which he'd known all his life – but one in which he had moved up a rung. No longer just the son of a small farmer, but a man of substance, with a farm, buying and selling land, a business, and a wife.

His first tragedy occurred that year; his wife, who also came down with the 'ague' as he had in the early days, gave birth to a boy who only lived ten days.

1792 also saw the beginning of what would become the great family exodus from Lyme to the Genesee. Colt's brother Samuel arrived – and didn't leave. In the end, all of Colt's brothers and one of his sisters came west, and all of Elizabeth's brothers. Two of his three brothers became merchants – and churchwardens – and in due course trustees of the school in Canandaigua, and in the case of Samuel co-manager of an early factory near Geneva, making clothing. The mass exodus of family networks further cemented the New England 'transplant'. Some of the larger households of the 1790 Census may well have been composed of sibling families, as well as servants.

Colt diversifies his enterprises

Colt's ways of making money were expanding. Not content just with the farm and land speculation, he also became a merchant: '... took with me from Lyme Samuel Landers, a Lad. At Hartford, I purchased of Elisha Colt [Judah's cousin, son of Harris] a quantity of Goods'; and 'at the opening of the Spring [1793] I again attended to my farming business, retailing Goods, and as often as occasion required executed the duties of the Office of Sheriff.'

He had enough capital by September 1793 to 'collect timber for a dwelling house and raised it and covered the same before the winter set in'. Mrs Colt was again 'the mother of a man child who lived about thirty hours.'

Mrs Colt (never Elizabeth) must have played a huge part, as all women did, in the farm and the settlement. The dairy, the kitchen garden, the weaving, bakery, dress making, preserving, cooking, the milking – all of this was her domain. Without it the farms would not have functioned. Before she arrived, a hired woman would have performed these tasks. And yet Colt never mentions this. Women, like Native Americans and slaves, remain as invisible on the frontier as they had been in Connecticut.

Colt's may have been increasingly prosperous with all his enterprises, but his wife was far from well. He took her to her parent's home in Lyme in April 1794. She was still in a feeble state of health. She would remain in Lyme, gaining strength, for a year. Colt took advantage of this trip back home to carry out 'business of Land Speculation'. He continued to make money on

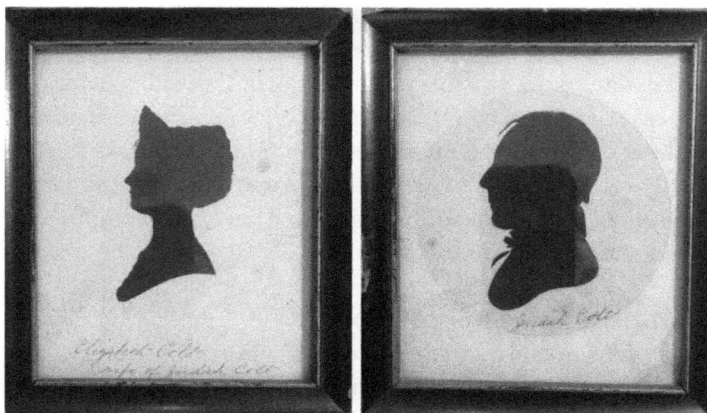

Figures 21 and 22: Silhouettes of Elizabeth and Judah Colt as young adults (in the possession of Herbert Spencer). Photograph by Margaret Spencer.

these journeys, buying and selling land, whether still merely notional – unsurveyed, a scrap of a paper warrant – or already settled with dwelling and clearances, on his own account or carrying out commissions for others. This was a lucrative way of making money. It was more lucrative than farming could be, when transportation was so rudimentary and risky – and expensive. The other promising 'sideline' was dealing in dry goods at his store in Canandaigua. With suppliers who would give him a good deal, provided Colt could find a good method of transportation, this was another source of wealth, a by-product of land settlement.

> I returned back to Canadaqua [Canandaigua, in 1794], where I spent the summer attending to my Store, farming business, Office of Sherriff, & employed sundry Mechanics to finish My House, & in the course of this Year I purchased sundry Tracts of Land, part of which I sold at an advance & what I retained has arisin greatly in value....
>
> I continued in Ontario until October, set out again for Connecticut, arrived at Lyme some time in November, found Mrs

Colt in better health than when I left her in the Spring. After a short visit set out again for New York, for the purpose of disposing of Land, succeeded in making sale of sundry Tracts, returned back to Ontario to transact some business with Arnold Potter & others, & after short stay, set out in the month of December again for New York ... [where] I made some sale on commission for Arnold Potter, which neated [sic] me a handsome profit. (*Narrative*)

Colt was now indeed playing his part in Nye's 'Second Creation', bringing goods from the East to sell to the new settlers, and using the new manufactures to clear the land and set up fields and farms where were forest and swamp. Blaakman has shown us 1780s and 1790s land mania on a grand scale, how the big firms and politicians bought and sold 'futures' in land and set up a pattern of imperial capitalism and settler colonialism that endures to our own times. In his *Narrative*, Colt weaves himself in and out of the picture Blaakman paints – of the speculator, investor, buyer of warrants, settler with secure title to his land, and part of the vast servicing infrastructure of importers, storekeepers, surveyors, and land agents which land mania spawned.

Colt played all of those roles at times, in these early years of the new Republic. It was his ability to fulfil all these roles that allowed him to climb the social ladder, that made him a sheriff, gave him the right to call himself 'Esquire'. He did what we would call networking – over huge distances, using introductions to gain himself an audience, doing business on behalf of others on the East Coast and back on the frontier. Men like him were essential to the big capitalists back east. Juggling the different roles he played entailed a lot of travel each year – physical travel – from the old world of Connecticut to the new frontier and the new US towns. It involved carefully nurturing social networks across the country. In this way he both climbed the social ladder and helped form civil society on the frontier in the image of the Anglo-American Colony of his youth.

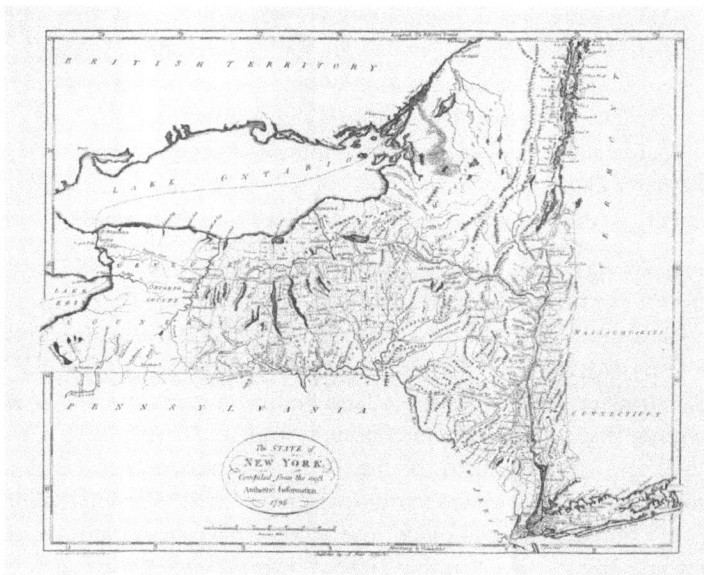

Figure 23: Detail, 'The State of New York Compiled from the most Authentic Information, 1796', six years after Colt's arrival in 'the wilderness'. Carefully ruled into rectangular townships, it tells a story of rapid westward expansion.[75]

In these first years, Colt brought oxen and horses from the East, and 'household necessities' which he bought from Elisha Colt – maybe on credit? Or at preferential rates? Back in 1790, Canandaigua had had access to just one sawmill – an absolute necessity for the frame houses, their floors, and garden fences; and a grist mill. By 1794 the town boasted shops, a blacksmith's, a courthouse. It had become a true County Town (of Ontario County) in only six years, an astonishing feat of settlement. As for Colt himself, from his first log house and barn (1790 and 1791 respectively), farming and 'retailing goods' mentioned early in 1793, to raising his second, grander house in 1793, as he said,

---

[75] https://legacy.lib.utexas.edu/maps/historical/new_york_state_1796.jpg

'every exertion was made to acquire property & lay foundation for an Estate' (*Narrative*). He had his wife and his brothers around him, and plenty of other New Englanders as neighbours. He had diversified his ways of making money. He was a person of standing in the County Town, probably much higher status than he could have achieved in Lyme.

The new country was being rapidly settled all around them. The 1796 map above shows so much – about the pride of the settlers and their obliteration of the Native Americans. Where just 18 years before there had been 40 First Nation villages (see the 1771 'Land of the Iroquois' map shown earlier), now only water – rivers and lakes – had First Nation names; everything else was named after people, places in New England, and prominent people of the Classical world – Ovid, Tully, Scipio. Open country had given way to the imposed grid decreed by Jefferson. This was empire-building indeed.

A salutary comparison:
The short-lived Williamsburg settlement

The civil society being created – or recreated – on the western frontier seemed to have stern boundaries. If you stepped outside these – by tending to luxury, or drunkenness, you stood out for censure. And European settlers simply didn't have the stamina or the nous. Towards the end of his time in Canandaigua, Sheriff Colt was sent a message by Governor George Clinton himself: there was news of rioting in Williamsburg, on the Genesee River to the west. Colt raised a posse – not easy given the few 'white' people living in Ontario county 1794 – to ride over and quell the rioters.

Williamsburg had 70 families – all Europeans who had been lured from the streets of Hamburg, Germany (i.e. none of them farming folk, and, reputedly mostly a 'bad lot' of city idlers and gamblers) who had been sold land by the London Associates land company. The Hamburg settlers travelled, at the company's expense, with farming implements, household utensils, and enough livestock and seeds to start their 70 farms – all this paid for by the company) and had arrived in Williamsburg the previous autumn.

The 'town' had been carefully prepared for them, with houses, tavern, mill and smithy, a minister of religion and a lawyer. Captain Charles Williamson, the company agent, himself a Scot, had thought all this necessary to attract settlers to such a backwater – in fact he had also arranged for a road to be built, not directly from Albany, but up through the Susquehanna, from Pennsylvania. He had even 'ploughed 80 acres of flats and built a long row of dwellings'.[76]

Orsamus Turner, writing over 50 years later, clearly regards this as European overkill – the absurdly and unnecessarily lavish preparation for a settlement, ruinously expensive and bound to fail. Carried out by a foreigner with more money than sense.

Turner also thought the choice of town settlers equally laughable and doomed from the outset – European town dwellers! No knowledge of farming! And the end of the story reads like a parable. The citizens of Hamburg (according to the story) had slaughtered the beasts for food, cooked the seeds, refused to clear and plough the land, and were carousing in the tavern – along with their minister. (Even the German religious leader was shown up in this account to be no good.) This choice of settler had been made by a Mr Colquohoun of the London Associates. Colquohoun had been duped, in Turner's view, into taking on this group of German idlers, regarded by their German sponsors as 'poor, industrious Saxons'.[77] When the Germans arrived, Turner tells us:

> Axes, spades and hoes were provided for them, and they set to work: and bad work enough they made of it. They had to be first taught the use of their tools, and were far from learning easily. An old gentleman who came over the road in an early day, says the trees looked as if they had been 'gnawed down by beavers'.[78]

---

[76] Turner, O. (1851), p. 254.

[77] Ibid., p. 254.

[78] Ibid.

Things went from bad to worse. The women were as improvident (note the word) as the men – making 'bad use of the provisions'. 'They fried their pork and then threw it away, supposing the grease only intended for use' according to one eyewitness. 'The whole fiddled and danced, and drank whiskey.' 'One stock of provisions was consumed and another had to be supplied.'[79] This could not go on.

Trouble eventually broke out when Williamson – who had left the whole undertaking with an employee, and was engaged in another part of the country – arrived back in Williamsburg and tried to create some discipline. Hence the riot. It seems that Williamson, his clerk, and the lawyer fled for their lives.

When Colt and his posse arrived, they managed to quell the rioters, and bring them back to face trial in Canandaigua (probably in the new Court House). In the event, fines were imposed but were not severe. Turner shrugs this off as a way to teach them a lesson about the rule of law. What it does expose is the problem faced by frontier societies where the gaols were a week's hard journey away to the east. Even then, the Germans couldn't find the money to pay these fines, so the fines were 'worked off' – as hours of labour amongst the settlers in Canandaigua. Meanwhile, the London Associates made a deal with the British in Canada, and sent the whole lot of Germans packing to Toronto.

The outcome of all this was the failure of Williamsburg: for years it remained in ruins. Colt would have drawn the moral: success had to be built on the hard work of serious and respectable New Englanders.

O'Reilly, too, 50 years on, was happy to use the story of Williamsburg to give his New York State readers an edifying lesson in why only a 'New-England character, as exemplified by the Pilgrim Champions of Human Rights' was up to the task of settlement – and that 'the transforming influence of Yankee

---

[79] Ibid., p. 255.

colonists in the western wilderness was required for this second creation'.[80]

Certainly, Captain Williamson, the Scot, did not fit the bill. On 23 September 1794, the same year as the trial of the rioters, the diarist James Emlen wrote:

> ... in the Evening we reached Bath, a Town begun by Captain Williamson about 18 Months since, which now contains perhaps 15 or 20 Houses. Capt. Williamson appears to be a Man of an enterprising Genius; yet pity it is that amid his extensive efforts for the settling of this Country he discovers a taste for Luxury, that Bane of happiness; we observed two of his horses leading along the Street of Bath swaddled in Blankets, which we were informed were training up for the races; it is astonishing how great [is] [the influence?] Men in conspicuous situations [blank] have on the Manners of a Neighbour[hood] if the settlers of this infant Country should imbibe a fondness for vain amusements it will greatly militate against their prosperity in every sense.[81]

Why didn't Colt mention the Williamsburg incident in the *Narrative*? It is possible he was not sure he'd handled it properly. But more likely, he was at pains, in his *Narrative*, to let as little as possible stain the picture he wished to portray of 'steady' New Englanders farming an 'entire new country'. This was the smooth, unmarred account he was creating and he would leave out any inconvenient events that got in the way.

*

---

[80] O'Reilly, H. (1838), p. 28: 'Those who properly appreciate the New-England character, as exemplified by the Pilgrim Champions of Human Rights and by their lineage from the first settlement down to the present period, may view with interest the living monument of intelligent ENTERPRISE which has sprung into existence through the transforming influence of Yankee colonists in the western wilderness.'

[81] Fenton, W. (1965), pp. 279–342, 288–9.

THE FIRST COURT HOUSE, ERECTED 1794.

Figure 24: Canandaiga's first Court House, raised in 1794.

In February 1795 Colt brought Mrs Colt and her sister back from Connecticut by sleigh only pausing to purchase 'a team of Oxen' at Pittsfield, and collect 'sundry dry Goods stored at Albany'. All was going to plan. Mid-1795,

> I continued to the business of my Store and farm until some time in August, when with Augustus Porter & Myself set out on a Journey to Presque Isle for the purpose of purchasing Land.

'Purchasing land' was one of his best way of making money. Leaving Canandaigua mid-season, in August, suggests that he had enough staff or relatives at home to run the store and the farm while he was gone. Porter, like Colt himself, was a surveyor. (Like Colt, Porter wrote a diary, published in 1904 by the Buffalo Historical Society.) But, as of yet , there is nothing to suggest Colt was thinking of moving to that part of Pennsylvania on the shores of Lake Erie.

Canandaigua is described by a traveller in June 1795:

... the houses, although built of wood, are much better than any of that description I have hitherto seen. They consist mostly of joiner's work, and are prettily painted. In front of some of them are small courts, surrounded with neat railings. There are two Inns in the town and several shops, where commodities are sold, and shoes and other articles made. The price of land here is three dollars per acre without the town, and fifteen dollars within.[82]

The price of land had increased from one to fifteen dollars per acre in six years. Colt's land speculation was indeed profitable. The architecture of the new Ontario County Court House in Canandaigua – New England to its core – shows clearly the aspirations of the new settlement. Progress indeed.

---

[82] Duc de La Rochefoucauld-Liancourt, quoted in Turner, O. (1851), pp. 175–6.

Chapter 6

To the Erie Triangle:
Land agent for the Pennsylvania
Population Company

Opening up the land south of Genesee country

What happened next in 1795, according to Colt's *Narrative*, stemmed from a decision 'concluded in my own mind' to 'change my line of business'. No mention of a discussion with his wife, and no real justification, so we are left to guess what happened. First, it is important to look at what was happening in the area of Pennsylvania that Colt and Porter had set off to reconnoitre – for land purchase.

The whole northern frontier country was facing problems. A couple of hundred miles south-west of Canandaigua, on the southern shores of Lake Erie, there were reports of much Native American unrest. Given the opinion we have seen that Canandaigua settlers had of the First Nation – 'scary', 'savages', 'brutal' – it is not surprising this gave cause for alarm. The Six Nations of the Iroquois were gathering, reportedly to try to prevent more US land settlement further west. They were led by one Captain Brandt – who had been in the British/Native American v. Clinton–Sullivan Patriots campaign in 1779 that had wiped out Seneca villages such as Canandaigua. Brandt was a Native American who had been raised by the colonists, been educated in Dartmouth College, New Hampshire, and was a freemason. Described as a 'man of two worlds', he was present at many of the early treaties with State and Federal authorities and Land Companies. However, to the new settlers in upstate New York this man was just another 'savage'.

The outbreak of hostilities was feared in the new settlements, and checked other settlers coming westward for a time. There were rumours of skirmishes with the Native Americans – 'much talk of Indian War with the Six Nations … serious apprehension of an invasion', as Colt records.

The reason for the unrest was a dispute over a particular part of the country which had been 'sold' to the State of Pennsylvania by the Federal government in 1792, and which Pennsylvania was immediately keen to have settled. The State had already (1792–4) gone a long way to map and sell the area. They called it familiarly the 'Erie Triangle' or 'Pennsylvania Triangle'; it was a triangular piece of land on the boundary between Pennsylvania and New York State. New York already had good lake access at Niagara to both Lake Ontario and Lake Erie. Pennsylvania did not. In the era of land mania, this 'triangle' was a prime piece of real estate. Pennsylvania had taken the prize, and with this additional acreage secured Lake access for itself – and a magnificent harbour at Presque Isle with its military fort. Colt writes in his *Narrative* that in 1794, 'Brant with his Warriors at Buffalo Creek was proceeding to Presque Isle, State of Pennsylvania to prevent the Surveyors from Surveying that part of the Country called the Triangle….'

But the fears had eventually been put to rest. As Colt informs his reader, early in 1794, Israel Chapin Esquire (who first gave Colt shelter when he arrived at Canandaigua in 1789), the Superintendent of Indian Affairs for the Federal government, met the 'Indians' with Samuel, Colt's brother – now part of the Colt enterprise in Canandaigua and formally employed by the government to record the event as Secretary, and Horatio Jones (who had been partly brought up by the Native Americans) as Interpreter. The surveyors of the Triangle went home, and Chapin arranged for a treaty to be held 'in the ensuing fall'. This treaty was sealed in 1794 in Canandaigua.

The Canandaigua Treaty of 1794 finally gave the promise of safety for those involved in the land business in the Erie Triangle.

President George Washington granted Native Americans the possession of their own reservations in New York State: Cattaraugus and Allegany on the shores of Lake Erie, and, near the Finger Lakes, Tuscarora, Tonawanda and Onondaga, each for a different nation of the Iroquois. The land agents, individual settlers, surveyors, began to go about their business again. This brought to an end the uncertainties and fear of war which had beset the Triangle lands since Pennsylvania took over the area in 1792.

Colt and Porter set out

So, in August, 1795, when Colt and Augustus Porter 'set out on a Journey to Presque Isle for the purpose of purchasing land', they did so in the belief that the way to settlement was finally open.

Porter was 26 years of age, Colt 33. They travelled by horse and boat. They found a fort (Presque Isle, previously a French fort on the peninsula), 100 US troops, and Andrew Ellicott laying out the town of Erie with Thomas Rees, agent for the Pennsylvania Population Company. Colt and Porter each bought 400 acres from Rees at 1$ an acre to 'pay in 5 annual instalments'. Colt's purchase was to be the site of his settlement Greenfield. In his entire journey, to Erie and back, there is not a single mention of Native Americans in Colt's *Narrative*, although we know they were there. Porter's record of the same trip does mention them – he explicitly tells us the trip took them through Indian territory:

> ... in company with Judah Colt. At this time all that part of the State lying west of Phelps & Gorham's Indian purchase was still occupied by the Indians, their title to it being yet unextinguished. There was of course no road leading from Buffalo eastward except an Indian trail, and no settlement whatever on that trail. We travelled on horseback from Conewagus [now Avon] to Buffalo, and were two days in performing the journey.[83]

---

[83] Porter, A. (1904), *Narrative of Early Years in the Life of Judge Augustus Porter*, Buffalo: Buffalo Historical Society Publications 7, p. 300.

Porter goes on to explain that the 100 militiamen at Erie were there to protect the surveyors against the Indians, despite the amicable settlement of the previous year. But Colt makes no such mention, rendering them invisible.

Colt records what happened after he returned to Canandaigua, which will have confirmed for him yet again that it was not a healthy part of the world:

> Shortly after my return home I was taken Sick with the bilious fever, which reduced me very low, was brought to the border of the Grave, but was raised up & restored to health, while I lay confined, Mrs. Colt, my brother Jabez & one of the domestics were sick with other complaints, but we were all preserved while others were taken away by death, Our sister Phoebe Merwen [Marvin] continued well and was attentive to our helpless state & rendered us much assistance for which I will always remember with gratitude. (*Narrative*)

This tells us many things. First, that illness was still a huge problem. Bilious fever – probably yellow fever – was a new danger, on top of the malaria, to add to the trials in New York State. Second, we see the household expanding : 'one of the domestics' suggests two or more. This is surely a step up in the world. Third, praise for a woman, who suddenly becomes visible, as a nurse. And fourth, this brush with death seems to have shaken Colt. He continues:

> I continued in Trade until some time in December, when concluding in own mind to change my line of business, I sold off all the Goods remaining in my Store to Thaddeus Chapin & others on a credit attended (?) to settle up accounts, and close all mercantile transactions, in which I was pretty successful.

From land speculator to land agent

'Change my line of business' suggests that he wanted to change definitively from a storekeeper farmer to concentrate on land speculation. This would involve setting up his own township, overseeing the development of other townships and farms he sold, aspiring to become the biggest fish in *his* 'purchase' as Phelps and Gorham had done in theirs. In Canandaigua Colt had been part of a settlement which had grown extraordinarily fast – a transformation from destroyed Indian villages and forest to land laid out in fields and settlements resembling New England, in six years. He was confident he could do the same, on his own account, pushing further south and west into what he called 'the wilderness'.

Colt seems to have conceived his plan after talking to the Pennsylvania Population Company land agent, Thomas Rees, in Presque Isle: he himself would purchase a large parcel of land in the Erie Triangle. After his reconnoitre with Porter, he had his eye on a part of the Triangle near to two important waterways – French Creek to the south and an inlet of Lake Erie to the north. Transportation was important to attract settlers. It was also important for marketing crops sown in the new settlements. The residents of Upper New York State were keenly aware at the time that their prices were uncompetitive with those in the East, once the transport costs were factored in. In any case, transport was uncertain and could take so long that perishable goods like grain could be spoilt *en route*. Colt will have had his eye on swift access via the waterways to Philadelphia via the Susquehanna and Ohio rivers, in addition to the route he knew along the Lake to Buffalo, Lake Ontario, and across to the Mohawk River. Going home to New York State and immediately succumbing to the fever will only have confirmed his ambition to move.

By late 1795 he had decided to buy as much as he could in the Erie Triangle. He saw an opportunity and was determined to carry out his plan to purchase a large tract of land with money from the sale of part of his Canandaigua property. He convinced other members of the family to join him. First, the family went to Lyme for the winter, as they often did, and then Colt set off for Philadelphia, then the Federal capital as well as the capital city of Pennsylvania, in order to effect a purchase. In early 1796,

> I returned back to Hartford on business, and in the month of March set of on horseback for Philadelphia, road as far as New York, where I left my Horse and took the Stage to Philadelphia, where I arrived the 13th inst [March]. The object I had in view was, to get confirmed the Land I purchased of Thomas Ren [Rees] agent of the of the Pennsylvania population Company at Presque Isle in August 1795 – the principal Proprietors of whom were residing in this City. I had it in contemplation also to purchase a body of land off the East end of the Triangle, so called, containing about 30000 acres & offered them one dollar per acre for the same, but they declined to sell in so large a body, while this proposition was under consideration of the Managers of Said Company viz John Nicholson Esquire, John Field, Theophilus Cazenove, Col. Aaron Burr. One of them viz Col Burr informed me they were in want of an agent to take in charge the sale of their Land – that if I would undertake the superintendence of their Land they would engage me, and upon a short consultation on the subject, I contracted with the Managers for one Year from the 21st Inst of March at a salary of 1500 Dollars & all expenses paid by them for Board, Traveling Expenses, &c, &c, – And Power of Attorney Letters were made out. Maps of the Country were furnished, & Money advanced to purchase provisions, hiring of Labourers, &c, &c. And in the month of April set out for the Geneseo Country, at New York laid in Stores of Provisions, sundry kinds of Goods, family & cooking utensils which are generally wanted in a New Country, shipped them to Albany thence across the portage in Waggons from thence they were taken in Battoes up the Mohawk River, through the Lakes to Presque Isle under the care and direction of Enoch Marvin. (*Narrative*)

This had not been Colt's plan. But his excitement at becoming a land agent rather than a land speculator is almost palpable.

Here were riches indeed. A salary, expenses, official legal status. Porter, as a chief surveyor of the Western Reserve[84] that year, only earned $5 a day for his labour; $1500 *and all expenses* was considerably more than this sum. And this was his opportunity to settle the area he had his eye on – the eastern part of the Erie Triangle – without having the risk of buying a vast amount of land himself. A land agent rather than an owner of the vast tracts of land he had dreamt of may have been a slight comedown, but on the other hand it reduced the personal risk – and, as it turned out, it increased the personal opportunity.

Colt made this a Colt family affair from the first – Enoch Marvin, whom he put in charge of transporting the goods, was his brother-in-law. Certainly he ran up bills with Elisha Colt in 1798: his *Day Book* has one entry for Elisha – owed $898.[85] Later on he also bought dry goods and utensils for the Company from Samuel Colt and Joseph Colt, two of his brothers then in partnership, back in Genesee country. His remaining brother Jabez also became a land agent in his own right with the PPC.

The Pennsylvania Population Company and the Holland Land Company

There were two giant land companies, both with Dutch backing, operating in this area – the Pennsylvania Population Company (PPC) and the Holland Land Company. One manager based in Philadelphia was a manager of both companies. Theophilus Cazenove, from Holland, had been sent from Europe to further the interests of all the shareholders. When he resigned in 1799, Paul Busti, originally from Milan, took over. The foreign investors had to engage US nationals to hold land for them – aliens could not hold legal title in Pennsylvania, unlike New York

---

[84] Around this time the Western Reserve, land on the shore of Lake Erie west of the Triangle, was sold by the State of Connecticut to the Connecticut Land Company.

[85] Judah Colt, *Day Book*; thanks to Beth Simmons, personal information, 2016.

– but the authorities were quite lax in prosecution. In 1792–3 the Holland Land Company was given seven years to get the ownership of their land into US hands.[86] The other members on the board of the PPC, Nicholson, Burr, Gibson, were national figures, whose life revolved around Congress, and State legislatures. They expected their land agents to do the real work, and paid them handsomely for doing it.

Colt was to learn a lot more in the next years about the 'gentlemen' who managed the PPC. John Nicholson had virtually bought the Triangle from himself, when as State Comptroller General he had first negotiated with the Federal government for Pennsylvania to buy the Triangle, and then, in 1792, 'just eleven days after the state had authorized the sale of these lands, Nicholson monopolized all 202,813 acres'.[87] This was the beginning of the Pennsylvania Population Company. Nicholson had engaged European money by involving the Dutchman Theophilus Cazenove, who had secured a lot of European money for the venture. European money – Old World money – was essential in these early years of the United States.

The 'pitch' of the Pennsylvania Population Company was in its name – it was to do the new Republic's job for it, populating the frontier lands, settling them to preclude or at least buffer any future invasion by Native Americans or the British. If it made a profit along the way, that was a happy event. For the State of Pennsylvania, the Company offered to take the risk of land sales, refill the State coffers, and do the dirty work of settlement. What could be wrong with this? The State did indeed recover its finances – by 1799 Pennsylvania's public finances showed a 'huge surplus'.[88]

Each of the 13 states behaved slightly differently, depending on how they were building their bureaucracies and laws. But

---

[86] Blaakman, M. (2016), footnote on p. 348.

[87] Arbuckle, R. (1974), p. 357. In fact, the acreage was more – 483,000 in the whole area, 202,813 in the Triangle and 297,813 further south-east in Pennsylvania.

[88] Blaakman, M. (2016), p. 266.

there is no doubt that the land companies – the big speculators – were a powerful influence in the new Republic. Between them they controlled more than 50 million acres of frontier land (for comparison this is twice the size of Pennsylvania and nearly as big as the entire United Kingdom).

Michael Blaakman describes this organic connection between the new State legislature in Pennsylvania and the speculators as a network of 'personal influence, public office, and individual relationships'. Land companies liked to claim that they were helping to do the State's work – a kind of private/public partnership. They would sell the land to settlers, often on long credit terms, supporting them with the necessary infrastructure of stores, mills, blacksmiths, civil life, while the State helped with grants for roads, and provided the legal and State organs – a militia, courts, representation in State politics.

This was the pattern followed by Phelps and Gorham in the Genesee country – in their efforts to get the land quickly settled, with the steady New England folk desired by Colt and his kind, they continued to treat with the Native Americans – giving them provisions, and cash. They also, on a personal level, engaged with the State, taking on positions as officials in the new settlements – both becoming judges, and putting significant money and land towards institutions – the County Court House in Canandaigua, the academy, and the turnpikes.

The land 'owners' in the Genesee in the 1780s had themselves taken an active interest in their settlements. While Phelps' main residence remained in Suffield, Massachusetts (until he lost all his money), he also had a residence of his own in Canandaigua, and suffered the rough life and rapid expansion of the frontier. But the later land 'owners' in Pennsylvania's Erie Triangle were a different breed. They had no intention of taking up residence themselves anywhere other than the big cities of the East. Many of the owners, in fact, were Europeans, dabbling in land futures, who lived in Amsterdam or London.

The land companies expected the untidiness of the

Pennsylvania land laws of the time to be smoothed over on the frontier itself. They thought problems could be got round by throwing money at them. The law stated your claim would be valid if you had a dwelling place erected and 2 acres of every 100 farmed within five years. The PPC were happy for land company agents to get their labourers to clear land in four adjacent corners of large plots and build simple houses on those four corners – thus making huge areas legitimate. The Company managers also hoped that, if there was any trouble from people who had cleared a patch of land back in 1792 or 1793 and came back after the troubles to settle, they could be removed by lawyers, by settlements out of court and so on.[89] There was to be trouble over this (see below). Arguably Quaker Pennsylvania was keener than New York to favour the small farmer, at least in its rhetoric, and to advocate Jeffersonian democracy. These differences were discussed in the Introduction.

Colt starts work with the Pennsylvania Population Company

By accepting Burr's offer to become land agent for the PPC, Colt found himself quickly embroiled in complications. He was to take over from Thomas Rees, whom he had met the previous summer.

Rees continues to have a part in this story. This is his 1795 description of the Erie Triangle before Colt took over:

... I sold as agent of the Pennsylvania Population Company, during that season, 79,000 acres of land, of which 7,150 acres were a

---

[89] Hale, N. (1949), p. 130: 'As a result of the complex nature of the Act of April 3rd 1792 which included two methods of acquiring title as well as a settlement clause, ' argues Hale – the Companies through long litigation kept the land titles in a state of uncertainty, the settlers weren't able to obtain absolute title in this section of the country, many settlers moved further west – he even argues 'Company ownership of lands retarded the development and prosperity of Northwestern Pennsylvania for many years.'

gratuity. The above quantity of land was applied for and sold to two hundred persons.[90]

While Rees was surveying in 1794 he had been alarmed for his life, after reports of white men killed on the Allegheny River by Native Americans, and had withdrawn. He had only come back in 1795 after receiving State assurances that he would be protected by troops. Rees had a double capacity – he was a land agent but also Pennsylvania State Deputy Surveyor – what we would now call a direct conflict of interest. Yet more complications.

Rees resigned both positions in 1795. In the end, the PPC were forced to pay him in land – 30,000 acres of it – in lieu of cash. 1797 saw Rees made a lifelong justice of the peace. This seems to have been in the PPC's interest – Rees was recorded as giving evidence on the side of the PPC and against 'adverse' or 'advance' settlers as late as 1806. (They are discussed below.) 'Adverse' suggests that those so described were in the wrong. 'Advance' suggests that they arrived first. Another use of language to make a point. Rees continued in the service of the State from 1796 to 1802 as 'commissioner for the sale of property in the County'. At both local and national levels, then, the network of personal influence, public office and individual relationships was strong. Like Colt, Rees was a Freemason.[91] Colt knew how to use his networks.

Colt arrived in the Erie Triangle in 1796. The legal requirements for Company and settler alike were a headache. A new land law in Pennsylvania in 1792 had made particular problems for speculators and their agents, and for settlers (see Introduction). But he did have a new title – land agent. And he did have a blank chequebook for necessary expenses. We know from Colt's *Day Book* that in 1798 these expenses amounted to more than $10,000. And he had his own network for buying

---

[90] Rees, quoted in Laura Sanford (1894), p. 78.

[91] Simmons, B. (2002) *Rees' Pieces*, Harborcreek Historical Society.

provisions, back east, which might help make profits for both himself and his extended family. (The *Day Book* also confirms this – Colt's 'upcountry' family gained over $1,000 that year.)

One of the land agent's responsibilities was to keep a daily journal. Although there is no record of his managers asking to see it, I assume that he – and they – felt they could ask to look at entries any time they wanted. This has consequences for us – and had for him. From 1796 we have copies of his *Journal* to help piece together his story. The *Journal* was written at the time, without hindsight, unlike the *Narrative* written more than ten years later. But the *Journal* entries themselves should be treated with special care – they were not written for himself alone, but with his managers (and their lawyers) in mind.

On 22 June, Colt erected his tent on Presque Isle and 'proceeded to business'. On 1 July 1796, his 35th birthday, his 'purchased goods', under his brother-in-law Marvin's care, arrived. In August he rode – rough going – to Pittsburgh 'as a vendor for the sale of part of the Erie Reserve' (another name for the Triangle) and he visited a fellow PPC land agent for the 'Company's Land on the waters of the Beaver'.

Of his travels there and back, he comments, 'Country new, but few Inhabitants, road bad and accommodations poor, encamped out nights, tied my horse head and foot.' No mention of Native Americans: the 1794 Canandaigua treaty had reduced risk from that quarter, and the defeat of Native Americans at Fallen Timbers the same year was definitive. [92]

Colt went back to Canandaigua along the shore of Lake Erie that summer– 'on horseback through the wilderness' – which we know meant him going through one of the largest Native American reservations, Cattaraugus, in New York State, although

---

[92] The Battle of Fallen Timbers, on 20 August 1794 near present-day Toledo in Ohio, was a tragedy for the First Nation. Their defeat opened the way for settlement of Ohio, and the Western Reserve: https://www.history.com/topics/native-american-history/battle-of-fallen-timbers, downloaded 10 July 2020.

this is not mentioned by him. After a brief stay, he returned swiftly to business in the Triangle where he stayed until 1 November. Now comes a new kind of problem for Colt: '... met with considerable opposition during the season by adverse settlers, a company known as Dunning & McNair, from the neighbourhood of Pittsburgh.'

On 4 November Colt left the Triangle via Canandaigua, where he stayed for a month, and 'by way of Albany & New York' to report everything to the Company's Philadelphia headquarters, leaving the land agency business in the Triangle in the care of Elisha and Enoch Marvin, his two brothers-in-law. Within months they were to move to begin the settlement of Greenfield.

Colt arrived in Philadelphia 1 January 1797. His managers were content to settle with him about the previous year's accounts and engaged him for another year with further 'Money to be laid out for the further prosecuting of the Settlement'. It was to be 'prosecuting' in more ways than one. He left Philadelphia on 5 March but did not reach Erie until May. His *Narrative* states that he was buying provisions, hiring men and purchasing cattle, but this sounds like a long leave of absence when his contract was annual.

He had one 'mishap' on his journey – worth a mention since he seems prejudiced against the effects of alcohol (especially spirits):

> 6-25th April busily employed in transporting Stores from Albany to Schenectady & shipping them again in Boats to Presque Isle – put them under the care of Eliphalet Beebe & others, except an accident haping to a large Boat, (in the care of Joseph Lesheer) upsetting in the Mohawk & a loss of about 25 barrels of Port – all business went on rapidly.

He admits to a 'hurry of business & anxiety to proceed on my Journey Westward' that prevented him seeing his sister Assenath, who was settled near Canandaigua, but otherwise seems to have assumed that his deputies were looking after everything for him adequately.

Colt arrived back in Erie on the 31 May 1797.

The very next day, 1 June 1797, Colt 'road out to where Mr Elisha Marvin was stationed and who had charge of the men imployed under my agency.' This was Greenfield, the spot he had marked out – 9 miles south of the Sixteen Mile Creek which ran into the Lake, and only a short distance from the navigable waters of French Creek. He and his brothers-in-law must have made their decision that this was a prime place to make their settlement. Waterways were crucial for transporting goods to the west, and now the Western Reserve was opened up by its sale to the Connecticut Land Company, there promised to be plenty of passing trade. The upland, so near the Lake, looked healthy as well as fertile. Calling the settlement 'Greenfield' showed how optimistic he felt.

According to an 1884 history of Erie County:

> The surface of Greenfield Township is mainly hilly, but there are some fine flats along French Creek and upon a tributary of that stream which comes in from New York at the southeast corner. Good for cattle, peaches, wheat corn oats flats all kinds of fruit potatoes. Up land best for grazing.[93]

The Erie County history goes on to say that, with the exception of Presque Isle and the town of Erie, the first white settlers in the area deliberately chose the uplands away from the lake, because the lakeside was swampy and heavily forested.

Waterways allowed good access at a time when roads were poor – not only to the North, near the headwaters of Six, Twelve, Sixteen and Twenty Mile creeks which ran into Lake Erie at those distances from the border with New York State, but also near the branches of French Creek to the south – that ultimately gave access to the Susquehanna and Ohio rivers. Roads were cut north and south by 1798. And waterways also provided sites for mills.

---

[93] Bates, S.P. et al. (1884), p. 782.

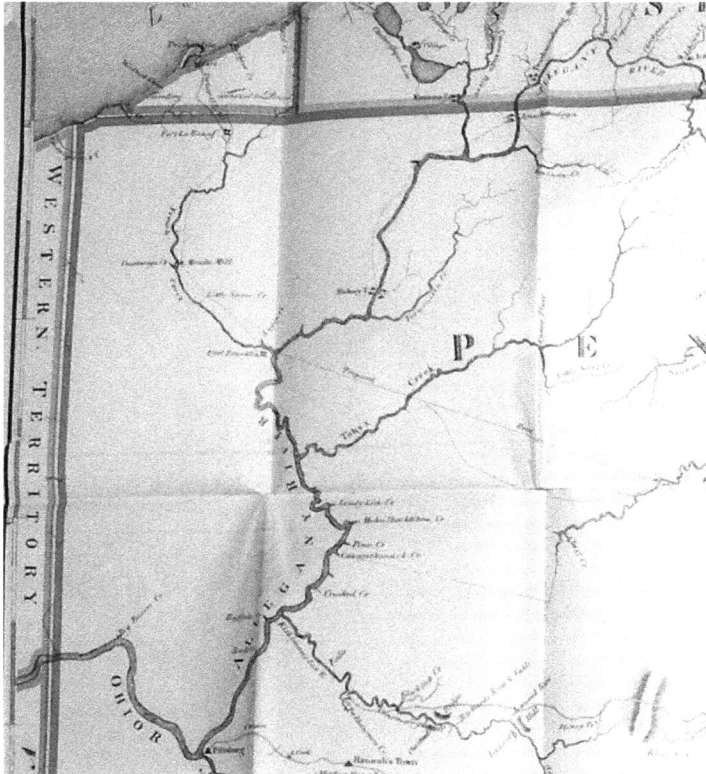

Figure 25: Detail from a 1791 map of Pennsylvania made by John Adlum and John Wallis.[94] It shows the navigable rivers that provided the way by boat from Eastern Pennsylvania to Lake Erie. At the top is the Erie Triangle ('Territory Annexed to Pennsa.'). French Creek was navigable up to the corner of the Triangle nearest to Greenfield. From there it was an easy portage to 'Harbour Creek' flowing into the lake. Top right is the Seneca village on Lake Chataqua (one of the villages not mentioned by Colt).

---

[94] https://www.google.co.uk/imgres?imgurl=x-raw-image:///a45c05cde 7df60792b8025d0920c23e1c0adc003d89f500b1de986a0881a7475&imgre furl=https://muse.jhu.edu/article/693339/pdf&tbnid=eWDf580FXKQ2J M&vet=1&docid=TXxLwbtkaXHVqM&w=513&h=835&source=sh/x/im, downloaded 11 December 2020.

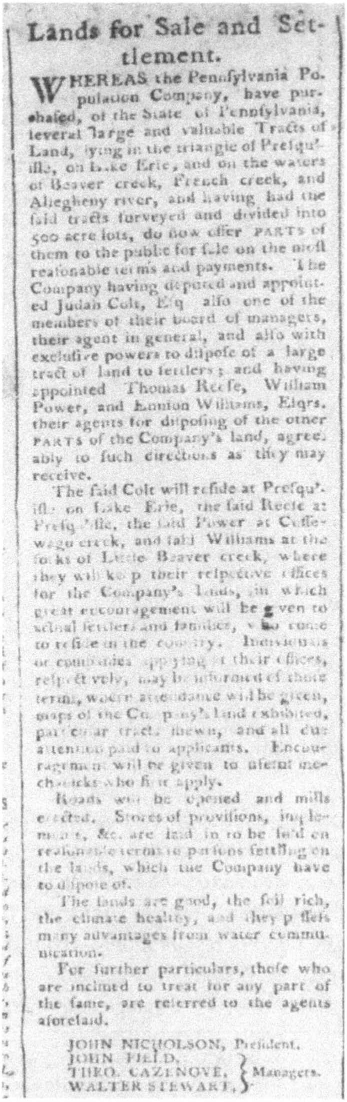

Lands for Sale and Settlement.

WHEREAS the Pennsylvania Population Company, have purchased, of the State of Pennsylvania, several large and valuable Tracts of Land, lying in the triangle of Presqu' isle, on Lake Erie, and on the waters of Beaver creek, French creek, and Allegheny river, and having had the said tracts surveyed and divided into 500 acre lots, do now offer PARTS of them to the public for sale on the most reasonable terms and payments. The Company having deputed and appointed Judah Colt, Esq. also one of the members of their board of managers, their agent in general, and also with exclusive powers to dispose of a large tract of land to settlers; and having appointed Thomas Reese, William Power, and Ennion Williams, Esqrs. their agents for disposing of the other PARTS of the Company's land, agreeably to such directions as they may receive.

The said Colt will reside at Presqu' isle on Lake Erie, the said Reese at Presqu'isle, the said Power at Cussewago creek, and said Williams at the forks of Little Beaver creek, where they will keep their respective offices for the Company's Lands, in which great encouragement will be given to actual settlers and families, who come to reside in the country. Individuals or companies applying at their offices, respectively, may be informed of their terms, where attendance will be given, maps of the Company's land exhibited, particular tracts shewn, and all due attention paid to applicants. Encouragement will be given to neat merchants who first apply.

Roads will be opened and mills erected. Stores of provisions, implements, &c. are laid in to be laid on reasonable terms to persons settling on the lands, which the Company have to dispose of.

The lands are good, the soil rich, the climate healthy, and they possess many advantages from water communication.

For further particulars, those who are inclined to treat for any part of the same, are referred to the agents aforesaid.

JOHN NICHOLSON, President.
JOHN FIELD,
THEO. CAZENOVE, } Managers.
WALTER STEWART,

Figure 26: Advertisement placed by Pennsylvania Population Company in the Pittsburgh Weekly Gazette, 10 June 1797.

A few days after Colt's arrival in Greenfield, on 10 June, the PPC advertised in the *Pittsburgh Weekly Gazette* 'Lands for Sale and Settlement':

> several large and valuable Tracts of Land, lying in the triangle of Presqu'ille, on Lake Erie, and on the waters of Beaver creek, French creek and Allegheny river ... deputed and appointed Judah Colt, Esq, also one of the members of their board of managers, their agent in general, and also with executive powers to dispose of a large tract of Land to settlers; and having appointed Thomas Reese, William Power and Ennion Williams, Esqrs, their agents for disposing of the other PARTS of the Company's land.

The notice continued: 'The lands are good, the soil rich, the climate healthy, and they possess many advantages from water communication.'

Colt stayed in the Triangle until November 1797, making trips to Meadville, and leaving – yet another family member – his brother Jabez Colt in charge of the PPC agency for the land on the waters of the Beaver. And, we assume, all paid from 'necessary expenses' by his managers.

'Advance' or 'adverse' settlers: Claim and counterclaim

But, there was a snag. We have already heard about the problems encountered earlier by Rees in the Triangle. There was no plain sailing, no easy selling of tracts of land on terms to settlers as in Canandaigua – all was frustrated by farmers already working the land who claimed the land was legally theirs. Later Colt was to recall this whole period:

> This was a season of much business and owing to the opposition I met with from adverse settlers, it caused me much trouble & perplexity, how to keep from 40 to 80 & 100 Men in the service of the Company to defend the Settlers & the property I had the charge. It was more than once Mobs of men from 20 to 30 would assemble for the purpose of destroying houses & for other

mischief, many of whom I had indicted, & bills were found against them by the Grand Jury of the then Allegheny County, the Court being held at Pittsburgh Borough. (*Narrative*)

This must have been a deal more expensive than the PPC had anticipated, as well as much more difficult for Colt than he had hoped. Nothing he had experienced in Canandaigua could have prepared him for this.

The special difficulty for Colt would have been the company he was forced to keep. It is hard to ignore any neighbour in an 'entire new country'. Especially neighbours who question your right to be there, and claim their precedence. Yet that is exactly where Colt found himself. Men had settled on land which the PPC now claimed belonged to it. And these settlers were not New England yeomanry. They were first generation Irish. And they were not just 'individuals'. They were connected to a small land company from which most had bought the land, Messrs Watt & Scott, with lawyers of its own, and had the power of a collective. Colt denounces them in his *Journal*[95] with a heavy display of prejudice, using the terms 'Mobs' and 'Mischief''. On his arrival, on 31 May 1797, he writes:

Informed of a violent opposition made by Messrs Watt & Scott, by their Agent William [?] Miles in preventing the Settlers of the Population Company from prosecuting their settlement – from this time forward had to encounter Many difficulties attended with Care and perplexity.

But nonetheless, these were neighbours. They needed to face common dangers together – whether wolves, or bears, or the threat of Native Americans, or sickness, or provisions; neighbours had to get on together. Colt needed their help. He continues:

Tarryed all Night at James Lowreys ... at 16 Mile Creek Thursday Morning on my arrival last evening I counted out and put in the hands of Mrs Lowrey 240 Dollars in Silver to keep until called for.

[95] Colt started his *Journal* in 1796.

Mrs Lowrey kept the tavern in the area. She was the mother of a group of brothers who had settled themselves on land they'd purchased from Watt & Scott. They were not Colt's kind of 'gentlemen' and nor were they labourers or artisans. They were farmers, who had fought in the War of Independence, self-made men with a background in Irish farming, who Beth Simmons, the Erie historian, describes as 'handsome bachelors'.[96] They and their friends and extended family, which included Barrs and Wilsons, had already started farming their plots. Now James Campbell (also Irish) and William Miles (agent of Messrs Watt & Scott) joined forces with the Lowrey clan in order to resist Colt.

They had good reason. In 1785, 12 years previously, Miles and Watt had painstakingly surveyed 'donation lands' (land given to veterans of the War of Independence) that lay north of Franklin, up to the New York State line (see map by Ennion Williams below). It took them two years. Miles, an Irishman had been asked by the Pennsylvania State governor to undertake the surveying of this area. When the land came up for sale, on behalf of Watt & Scott Miles bought the land and proceeded to find settlers. Some of this land was the same land that the Pennsylvania Population Company now 'owned'. Pennsylvania had employed different surveyors to map out different areas at different times, with the result that, on the ground, the lines had been drawn, the boundaries notched in trees, in ways that overlaid each other. Colt was no stranger to mild differences in surveying work, from Ontario County, but he was used to these being amicably sorted, lines redrawn, money exchanged, no harm done. But this was a different matter. The Lowreys and others had built cabins, cleared land, made a settlement near the Lake – and were faced with PPC men, hired labourers, clearing land and erecting dwellings and mills on land they were certain was theirs.

---

[96] Simmons, B. (2016), *The Lowry Clan*, Erie County (PA), Genealogy, Family Histories.

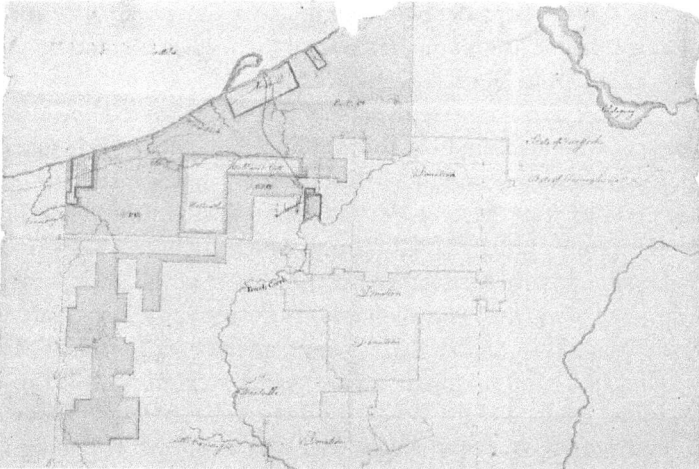

Figure 27: Part of a map drawn by Ennion Williams in 1800, when working as Deputy Surveyor for Pennsylvania. It shows land of the Pennsylvania Population Company ('P P Co') and the Holland Land Company ('Holland Coy'). 'Donation' is land donated by Pennsylvania to soldiers of the War of Independence. The two forts of Presque Isle and Leboeuf are marked and settlement of Meadville, but not Greenfield or Erie.[97]

The map drawn three years later by Ennion Williams, another man working for the State one minute and the land companies the next, gives a small indication of the complicated patchwork of problems faced by settlers at the time.

So here were settlers, who had bought land in good faith from one company, being threatened with eviction by another. A different agent might have made his peace much earlier with the families, accepting them as bona fide settlers, waiving the costs in return for working together on the new settlement. But Colt chose to start proceedings. The result was, predictably, threats and violent opposition through the whole of June 1797. From the *Journal*:

---

[97] James Gibson Papers, Historical Society of Pennsylvania.

Friday morning, at 16 mile creek, was called on by James Campbell, who informed me that if I did not desist in prosecuting the settlement under the Population Company, he should very shortly come forward with sufficient Number of Men to destroy whatever might be done by me.... replied, I did not mind his threats neither would they prevent me from Settling the County.

Colt was sufficiently alarmed by this threat to ride off through rain and mud to Erie to ask the advice of Rees, now the local deputy surveyor for the State. He came back the following day, 17 June, resolved to resist. On 19 June he wrote:

... our Infant Settlement was much disturbed by an Infamous gang of about 40 Men, headed by James Campbell & Thomas Miles who pulled down & destroyed several houses of the Companys Settlers.... intention was to done more mischief by demolishing the Store house & other building at the Station [Greenfield, later called Colt's Station] but finding them well garded relinquished the attempt.

He was informed they would try again, so resolved to employ about 40 men - to clear land and defend the settlement when needed. There was no local militia to help him out, so he wrote:

Mechanics busily imployed making weapons of defense, spears with a socket in which is placed a handle of wood not unlike a Spontoon to be used in case of an attack from these Buffeons as we are not supplied with Rifles, nor any other kind of firearms.

The language here expresses Colt's frustration but also displays his prejudices. Infamous gang, mischief, and most of all 'buffoon' portray in the language of the time the opposite of gentlemanly behaviour - it suggests wanton aggression, idiocy, 'mob' behaviour. In 1797 (this is from the *Journal*), in the era of the French Revolution, Colt's words were chosen to conjure the righteous - armed with ploughshares into spears - fighting off the unrighteous. He hammered this point home a few days later on 28 June when he wrote of the 'Bandittos' (Mexican bandits) and added that James Campbell liked to drink 'grog' – Campbell came to call on them not for the first time:

> ... was again called on by James Campbell an assistant agent of Watt & Co, & again threatened to destroy our Settlement, but finding his threats did not disconsert us – he took leave after supping at a little Brandy Grog, a kind of strong Water he was very fond of taking copious Drafts of.

Colt records with sadness that on that same day, 28 June 1797,

> after noon 3 Men of respectability arrived from Westmoreland (State of New York) to purchase land but on account of the opposition, of the advanse [here the transcriber typed over adverse to make it read advanse] party were discouraged from purchasing.

Here were settlers of the kind Colt hoped for – only for them to be turned away by what they witnessed.

But Colt was determined to work hard to get the kind of settlement he wanted. Here are two *Journal* entries from that summer:

> 12-15 June: All hands employed in making Roads, building houses, clearing land, erecting a Smith Shop, burning Coal, exploring land &c.

> 3 July: 16 Labourers returned from the woods whose business had been, in erecting Houses on vacant tracts

To protect the interests of the PPC, Colt cultivated the lawyer Thomas Collins, who frequently appears in his *Journal* – in Colt's house in Greenfield, and Collins' house in Pittsburgh – at social events with wives and sleigh rides.

Collins was first brought in during that summer. Colt had asked for him urgently on 5 June but he only arrived on 19 July. By that time Colt must have been desperate. On that day a Joseph Prescott began to raise a sawmill on 16 Mile Creek, where the Lowreys kept their tavern. But, 'Same day Prescott was forbid working by James Lowrey & others. Collins and Colt set to work.

> 20th July. The Day was taken up in writing & taking affidavits relating to the Riotous Conduct of the Intrusions of sundry of Miles & Men employed by him – two Writs of Ejectment, ware served this day one on Daniel Marsh & other on Henry Gilmore the latter (viz) Gilmore was Taken for one of the Rioters – the Lowreys conducted very riotously at the 16 Mile Creek by assaling Captain Beebe [Colt's friend from Connecticut and later the builder of the sloop *Washington*] & others with him who ware cutting timber for a small Vessel – also by throwing down the body of a Store house which had been erected at the Mouth of Creek – in the fray Beebe was much hurt by being struck with a Gun by James Lowrey, who is as grate a Rascal as ever escaped from Ireland (not hung) & all his brothers are not a whit behind him – whose Conduct will allway keep Society in a tumult. Unhappily for Pennsylvania thare are but too many people among them of that Nation to be long quiet & happy under the best of Governments.

> 22nd Saturday, a tumultuous, riotous day, at Evening Shipped off sundry of the Lowrey and his gang in boats to the Town of Erie – a scuffle insued on thare going on board of the boats – in which number of women ware very active in throwing Sticks & Stones.

The 'shipping off' was doubtless with the assistance of some of the 'from 40 to 80 & 100 Men in the service of the Company'.

Colt's attempts to contain the uprising didn't work. Thomas Miles and others went to the Lake to rescue the Lowreys from the hands of officers (as it afterwards appears) 'between 20 & 30 of them assembled with arms & Clubs at James Lowrey & spent the day in Drinking and rioting'.

Things were coming to a head. Colt had to go to oversee the other PPC settlement, Meadville, but left Greenfield well defended – just as well, because as he set out, a band of men under Thomas Miles rode up, destroying buildings as they went.

But finding Greenfield well defended, they withdrew. According to Colt both sides 'discharged their pieces' into the air or the trees before falling back. There were many arrests that summer. Cases were heard at the court in Pittsburgh:

'5th Sepr Tuesday, the principal part of this day was taken up with the Grand Jury, with the witnesses, to prove those complaints, of Riotous conduct of Miles Lowreys & their Connections & bill found against them.' [The *Journal* omits what penalties were handed down.]

This was a short-lived victory.

Over the next year Colt pursued his activities in Greenfield, Meadville, the Geneseo, Pittsburgh and Philadelphia.

On his birthday, 1 July 1798, he wrote:

My birthday, which brings me to be 37 years of age, no one year since my arrival at Manhood, that wisdom, or patience was required [to such an extent] than in the business of my Agency. ...

4th July Tuesday, being the Anniversary day of the Independence of America 22nd Year. l gave at the expense of the Pennsylvania population Company, an entertainment to about 75 people, settlers of the said Company, a bour [bower] was erected under two large Maple Trees, where their hearts ware cheered with goodfair. Sundry Tosts were drank sutible to the occasion. After l had withdrawn from the Table, One Frederick Crawford (a Dutchman) drank a Tost to this effect – May Judah Colt agent to the Population Company drive the Intruders of the Watt & Milestes before him as Sampson did the Philistines of Old Three cheers, and the wood rang, with a war of laughter for some time.

In 1800 the courts ruled in Watt's and Miles' favour and against the PPC, by which time Greenfield had become a thriving community that contained many of the 'intruders' living and farming alongside those who had bought their plots from Colt. Hale, in his work on the Pennsylvania Population Company tells us that the State land office in 1800 ruled in favour of the intruders over companies. Colt, by then had already 'compromised with the leading intruders'. Watt & Scott were paid $3,500; the MacNairs were lent $23,000, and given a half interest in 232 tracts in Erie County.

The painful story of claim and counter-claim is detailed in the works of Bates (1884) and Sanford (1861, 1894). But there it is explained away as a result of poor surveying – 'several provoking errors' in the Watt and Miles expedition in 1785, compounded by the spider's web of land laws passed by the State which allowed a multitude of claims and counter-claims to enter the courts. The real story is more painful, and less a forgone conclusion.

At court, the big land companies claimed the year 1796 was as unsafe for settlers as the previous three, because there had been the murder by Native Americans of a Mr Rutledge. The counter-claimants – smaller companies like Watt & Scott – claimed that the murder was not by a Native American ('Indian') but was by a white settler and was being falsely used by the big companies to gain advantage. The issue went back and forth in the courts of Pittsburgh and Philadelphia, becoming a political football between the Federalists (for the big companies) and the Democrats (for the small farmers and smaller companies). It was largely settled years later in 1802, when the Supreme Court of Pennsylvania ruled in favour of the big companies, and against the 'adverse settlers'.

Conflict on the ground continued after this second judgement. There are entries in both *Journal* and *Narrative* in which Colt and others attempt repossession of land and property in and near Greenfield, with varying success. Here is one from 22 August 1803:

> Road down to Tuttle's Mills, on my arrival there, saw Col. Timothy Tuttle and Mister Putman on horse back and Peter Kain by them, who informed that Sam'l Lord and Enoch Marvin had succeeded that morning in taking possession of Alexander Lowrey's House & also to take John Lowrey. I proceed on towards

Alexander Lowrey's House, in coming within about 40 purches of the House met Lord & Marvin who informed me that John Lowrey had made his escape, we however went back to the house found Alexander Lowrey's Wife, James Lowrey's Wife & their Mother Margaret Lowrey in the House, ordered them to clear the House which they did & put Mister Putman in possession. The Household goods were taken away by Peter Kane.

It was a sad ending for the Lowry family. John Lowry hung himself, another Lowry went to prison (though he was released when his wife went to Philadelphia to plead for him), and most of the family moved from Greenfield over the New York Line to Chataqua Lake.[98]

The sloop *Washington*

In 1797, Colt extended the company's involvement in the transport business: 'Commenced the building of a small vessel about 35 tons at the mouth of the 4 Mile Creek' (the nearest Lake inlet to Greenfield). This was the sloop *Washington*, part-owned by the PPC in whose name it was operated until 1800, when it was sold, because accounts showed it was losing money. But in 1797 it was yet another of those running costs the Philadelphia-based managers were asked to swallow. Colt felt himself flush enough to start this new enterprise. We know he had brought a boat builder with him on a previous trip from Connecticut, one Eliphalet Beebe. He set out, in 1797, to raise money from others to sink into building the boat, with the idea of using it to ferry people and goods back and forth from Niagara to the Triangle. At a time when Colt still had high hopes of the French Creek navigation making a simple portage possible from Philadelphia to the Great Lakes – via Greenfield – this seemed a brilliant venture. Here is a letter to Dunning MacNair from Colt the following summer of 1798, two months before the boat was launched, asking him to make good his offer of investment in

[98] Simmons, B. (2016).

the project. This is the same Dunning MacNair with whom he had been at odds at the outset of his land agency.

Meadville 14 July 1798

Col Duning McNear

Dr Sir,

I flattered myself of the pleasure of Seeing you in this Quarter before this time, with your good Lady and Famaily, butt am much disappointed.

I arived at Erie with my Famaily the last of May and am Now living at the Station I resided at the last Season. Mrs Colt is well pleased with the Country and as yet enjoys good health. I am going on Rapidly with the Vessel at the 4 Mile Creek it will be ready for Launching the first of September, I Purchased all the Sails & Rigging, Iron Tar Nails &c. at New York, and every other Article Appertaining which was Necessary to lay in, in that Quarter.

As there Was No Written Agreement between us, in regard the Building of Said Vessel, I am At a loss to Know what Share (if any) you wish to hold in her. She will Cost when ready to Sail About two thousand dollars. I have Advanc'd Already towards her one Thousand Dollars, principally in Cash. I have divided her into Eight Shares and reserved for you two of them, which will Cost, Say 250 Dollars pr Share, Equal to 500 Dollars the two Shares, if you are desirous to be Considered a Partner with me as formerly proposed you will please write me by my Brother Jabez Colt the Bearer of this whom I beg leave to Introduce to you and by whom I have taken the Liberty to draw on You for one hundred and Fifty Dollars on Account of the said Vessel and if Convenient and Agreeable to your Ideas being Considered a Share holder you will please to honour the Draught, and it shall be placed to Your Credit.

Whenever I hear of your Arrival at Coneout Shall make it a point to Call and See you on Account of those interferences with those Persons who Articled under me in 1796 for the Settling those Lands in your Quarter, a few of Which Tracts have Since been disposed of by you in 1797, a

Business which Ought to be Attended to as Soon as we Can, with Convenience – and what would be Very Gratifying to me would be to have the pleasure of waiting on you at my Station at Mount Pleasant.

Mean time I am with respect

Sir your most Ob[edient servant]

Judah Colt[99]

There are several aspects of this letter to catch the eye. First, like any good entrepreneur, he is out to attract capital – in this case from an enemy turned colleague, Dunning MacNair. Second, the tone of the letter and its content emphasize the social connections – wives, visits – which confirm how much Colt is relying on social networking. He sent the letter via his brother, hoping to obtain cash that way, securely. Third, his aspirations are spelt out loud and clear in calling his house 'Mount Pleasant'. And fourth, this looks like a business he contracted on his own account and then sold to the Company, who only took over the boat in October 1798.

The sloop lasted barely five years. Over 200 years later, its wreck was salvaged, and its story written up. The *Washington*

was the first ship built [by the new settlers] on Lake Erie and the first to sail in both Lakes Erie and Ontario. Construction of the sloop *Washington* began in 1797 on 4 Mile Creek by Connecticut carpenter Eliphalet Beebe for the Pennsylvania Population Company, an organization that was developing a tract of land just north of Erie, Pennsylvania. The *Washington* was a small sloop with a carrying capacity of 36 tons. The sloop was initially built to transport people, their belongings and needed supplies from the southern end of the portage from what is now Chippawa, Ontario

---

[99] Silveus, M. (1935) 'McNair correspondence: Land problems in Northwestern Pennsylvania', *Western Pennsylvania Historical Magazine* 18, p. 244.

around Niagara Falls. On September 15, 1798, the sloop was launched just north of the present city of Erie, PA. Its maiden voyage was to Fort Erie for supplies. The Pennsylvania Population Company took ownership of the sloop a month later on October 12th. Two names were proposed for the sloop, *Washington* and *Lady Washington*. The name *Washington* was chosen by the ship's largest shareholder, Robert Hamilton, a merchant from Queenston, Ontario. It appears, however, that the sloop continued to be referred to as *Lady Washington* by some.

For the next three years the *Washington* sailed the eastern end of Lake Erie, making frequent trips to Fort Erie [Presque Isle] and moving merchandise and settlers between New York State, Canada and Erie, Pennsylvania. By the end of the season in 1800, it was determined that the operation of the sloop was actually losing money and it was put up for sale. In November 1801, the *Washington* was sold to a group of merchants from Queenston, Ontario. Not long after, she was wrecked; she has recently been salvaged from the lake by divers.[100]

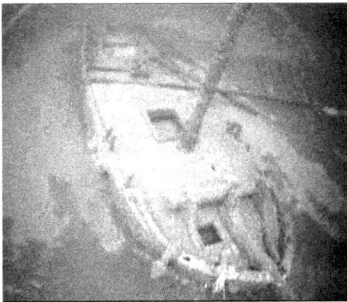

Figures 28–29: The sloop *Washington*. Photograph of wreck from bow to stern, by Roger Pawlowski; watercolour by Roland Stevens of Rochester, New York, painted after the wreck was found.[101]

[100] 'Rare 18th century sloop Washington discovered in Lake Ontario', *Great Lakes Scuttlebutt*, 24 August 2016.

[101] https://www.shipwreckworld.com/articles/gallery/120/483, downloaded 1 January 2021.

*

As well as a lawyer, and investing in transport, Colt got the company to allow him a clerk – Benjamin Saxton – to help with the business. And he secured a massive increase in his own salary – from $1,500 to $2,500. From Colt's point of view these were all reasonable expenses in the interests of doing his job – making certain the land owned by the Pennsylvania Population Company was settled, lot by lot.

The PPC boasted to their shareholders, back in Holland and France, that there could be a 200 per cent increase in your funds after 10 years. The way to reach these predicted profit margins was for settlers to come, and stay, and improve the land, taking their farms 'on terms', paying the company back with interest over a decade or more.

To make this happen, settlers had to be secure, have access to protection, to equipment, to mills, to transport, to a 'community' where their children could be schooled and they could enjoy good neighbours, barn raisings, help in times of sickness. Colt saw this as his business. And saw the company funds as his resources to make this happen. Colt had already seen failure, at Williamsburg in Ontario County.

Chapter 7

Judah Colt – Esquire

In this chapter, I use Colt's *Journal* to demonstrate the final touches to this transformation, and to observe his methods. He had shrewdly used the years of land mania to make money by buying and selling land on his own account, and gained status by doing the same as a land agent. He became a retailer, making use of the family storekeeper connections in New York, Geneva and Canandaigua. He laid out farms in Ontario County, New York, and in Erie County, Pennsylvania, and rented them out, becoming a substantial landlord. He had his own farming business, with arable land, orchards and livestock. And, to his own satisfaction, he remained a cultured, steady, New Englander, who could afford indentured servants, frequent travel to the East Coast, and a home life of hosting friends and passing dignitaries, philanthropy and religion. He was a New Englander steeped in English culture, English prejudices, English social patterns. Colt was able to live in the style of a gentleman because of his salary – and his 'expenses'. He retained his land agent's salary of $1,500 well into the new century – for one or two years he was even paid $2,500.

We learn from his *Journal* of his engagements – barn raisings, religious gatherings, of the travel conditions, and time spent in Philadelphia, Pittsburgh, Canandaigua and Connecticut. He tells us his views on politics, and waxes enthusiastic about new farming methods. We learn about the weather, and his harvests. He puts in writing who he hired, or lent money to, sold land to, or entertained. He recounts the trials of intruders, adverse settlers, settlers who can't pay, and all the measures he took to protect the Company he worked for.

We are also fortunate to have a third document, in addition to the *Journal* and the *Narrative* – Colt's *Day Book* (the PPC company expenses book) for the one year 1798–99. It was found in the late twentieth century, in an attic near Greenfield (now known as Colt's Station). As Beth Simmons writes:

> The 'Judah Colt Daybook – 1798–1799', a treasure to the historians of Erie County, exposes a high-tech society at Colt's Station in 1799, not the primitive log cabin wilderness society pictured for so many years in the Erie County history books. The men of the Pennsylvania Population Company were developers, not pioneer settlers. They used the finest equipment they could import, hired very talented hard workers, and quickly created an up-to-date environment in which to raise families.[102]

There are three late nineteenth-century books on the history of Erie County, written to glorify the region's first settlers (by now recalled as 'pioneers'): Laura Sanford's *The History of Erie County, Pennsylvania* (1861,1894), the *History of Erie County, Pennsylvania* by multiple local authors (S.P Bates et al., 1884) and Robbins's *Popular History of Erie County, Pennsylvania.* [103] With the help of these, and of more recent local historians keen to rediscover all the settlers, not just those from New England, we can trace too the disappointments and barriers he faced along the way.

In 1798 Elizabeth joined Judah in Greenfield, and they moved into a fine house which he had built – colonial style – two storeys, five windows upstairs, two either side of the front door. A central chimney ensured the house was warm all winter, with fireplaces in each room. Beth Simmons describes the construction:

---

[102] Simmons, B. (1997).

[103] Sanford, L.G. (1861), *History of Erie County, Pennsylvania*, Philadelphia: J.B. Lippincott & Co., enlarged and privately reprinted, 1894; Bates, S.P. et al. (1884) *History of Erie County, Pennsylvania*, Chicago: Warner, Beers & Co.; and Robbins, D.P. (1895), *Popular History of Erie County, Pennsylvania*, published in Erie.

Colt's house, a colonial five bay two story center-fired clapboard stood on the northwest corner of the present intersection of Pennsylvania State Routes 430 (Station Road) and 89 (also called Station Road). It was built by master carpenters Joshua and Sampson Hamilton, aided by James Henton, the main handyman of the settlement. Henton spent ten days laying the solid cherry floor in the house. He also laid a floor in the 'office', made a dining table for the kitchen, built a wheel barrow and an axle tree for a cart, spent seven days building two cart bodies and 2 1/2 days rimming the wheels for the carts and getting the timber for six pair of cart wheels. Another handyman, Joel Andrews, made '20 lights of sash' for the kitchen in June and in October was paid for making another 72 window lights and setting the glass in the sashes for the house.[104]

By the time of the 1800 Census, there were four adults living in this house and one youngster between the ages of 10–16, so three people in addition to himself and his wife. This house was the first house he built in Erie County – it survived until the early twentieth century, when it fell into ruin.

The 1884 history of Greenfield states:

Mr Colt took up permanent residence in 1797, having been preceded by Elisha and Enoch Marvin (his brothers-in-law), Cyrus Robinson, Henry and Dyer Loomis, Charles Allen, Joseph Berry, John and William Wilson, James Moore, Joseph Webster, Philo Barker, Timothy Tuttle, Silas and William Smith, Joseph Shadduck and John Daggett (each accompanied by his sons), and John Andrews. All of these were hardy and intelligent New England people.[105]

---

[104] Simmons, B. (1997). The Hentons (Hintons) have lived in Harborcreek Township since early settlement days. James Henton was the main handyman of Colt's Station.

[105] Bates, S.P. et al. (1884), p. 783. Buck, S. and E. (1949) also make the point about New Englanders being important in the early settlement of north-west Pennsylvania (p. 225).

Figure 30: Sign at Colt's Station, which Colt founded as Greenfield. A 'flatboat' is a bateau.

In Colt's day Greenfield was a busy place, being the depot of supplies for all the country round. For a year or two, the line of travel from the Lake was through Colt's Station to French Creek, and then on to Pittsburgh, a route that lasted until a good road was opened between Erie and Waterford. After Colt's departure, the glory of the station faded.[106]

By the time of the 1884 account, the Irish have vanished from the record altogether, along with the Native Americans. We see a successful New England colony of settlers, staying, industriously, for a few years, and then determining to move, when they saw better lands elsewhere, leaving only one of the old guard – Elisha Marvin, Colt's brother-in-law – to continue to farm. Colt himself remained a landlord of several farms in the area but that is not part of the 1884 history.

As we saw in the previous chapter, Colt's *Journal* and *Day Book* tell a much more turbulent story of the settlement of Greenfield, and a much more plausible reason for the failure of the settlement – now not much more than a crossroads with a diner.

---

[106] Bates, S.P. et al. (1884), p. 784.

The PPC calls Colt to account

Colt, though, had to stay for the first years, and see the Company interests served as best he could. The difficulties with 'adverse settlers' were compounded by another, more personal problem. Shortly after Colt brought his wife to join him and his two brothers-in-law in Greenfield in 1798, he was visited by a fellow surveyor of the area called Ennion Williams. Williams had worked for Thomas Rees as Deputy State Surveyor of the Triangle, and also for the Pennsylvania Population Company. He thus had two masters to serve, as well as his own interests. Williams was a Quaker, Pennsylvanian born, and a war veteran. He had watched Colt's progress, as he tried to secure Company lands by hiring men to intimidate the adverse settlers and effect a rapid settlement of land by getting his men to erect houses, clear lots, cut roads – anything to make the land attractive to the 'right' sort of settler to come and get the tracts on 'terms' – to pay back the Company with interest over a term of years. This may have seemed an extravagant course of action. Or Williams may have been himself prejudiced against 'gentlemen' from Connecticut. Or he may have watched with astonishment the raising of funds for the sloop *Washington*, the elegant house Colt built, the barrels of port – who knows. Whatever alerted Williams initially, in the end he seems to have found himself most troubled by Colt's extravagance.

Unknown to Colt, Williams called on the company managers in Philadelphia later in 1798 to alert them to his suspicions. They sent him back to keep an eye on Colt in Greenfield for the season of 1799; Colt was told to accommodate him. As we can deduce from the *Day Book* for 1798–9, which Beth Simmons has worked on, and from Colt's own *Journal*, transactions were for large amounts and in some cases more than a little opaque. Williams seems to have been right to be suspicious.[107]

Joseph Ellicott's accounts for the Holland Land Company,

---

[107] Simmons, B., personal correspondence about Colt's *Day Book*.

which were painstakingly transcribed by the Buffalo Historical Society and published in 1937, were meticulous.[108] But Colt's method of accounting is very different. Where Ellicott has a clear item against every dollar incoming and outgoing, Colt's *Day Book* accounts – which have some items like Ellicott's – peas or flour, beef or bread in specified amounts to a named person – have large amounts to one person or another not itemised. For example:

Stephen Hazeltine $1115.90½

Timothy Tuttle $850.48½

These large amounts may be entirely legitimate but since they are not itemised they may have raised the eyebrows of an already suspicious PPC manager. Colt's family loom large in the *Day Book* expenses columns. Here are a few examples:

Elisha Colt: Bills payable for cash paid for my note to Elisha Colt 15th May $849

Elisha Marvin for my acct his order $111.81

Elisha and Eno. Marvin for amot of their acct assumed $396.79

Jabez Colt to Cash paid himself $100

Judah Colt for private acct $38.47

Samuel Colt D to cash sent to New York 1000$

Enoch and Elisha Marvin $953.69

Colt lists family expenses for 12 gallons of brandy, 10 gallons each of sherry and port, and notes he has paid James Henton $8 for making him a dining table and $12 for spending eight days laying floors in his house. Were these legitimate expenses in the eyes of his managers?

---

[108] Robert W. Bingham (ed.) (1937), *Holland Land Company's Papers, Reports of Joseph Ellicott*, vol. 1, Buffalo Historical Society Publications no. 32, Buffalo. This collection shows much more what reports ought to look like – methodically kept.

Williams gave his report to the company directors in Philadelphia and Colt was duly summoned to give an account of himself. He was 'detained' (made to kick his heels) in Philadelphia for 13 months in 1800-1801. It was a visit in stark contrast to the one the year before, when he had gone up to the City with Mrs Colt for three months, and 'leisure hours were agreeably employed in attending the debates of Congress and Senate of the US – also the State Legislations, Federal Courts, &c &c.' This was the time of the Whiskey Rebellion – which Colt describes as an 'Insurrection with a RingLeader, and a Mob by a man by the name of Fries [who] was tried for high Treason, was finally condemned, but after was pardoned under the administration of John Adams'. This rebellion gives an indication of the politics of the 1799, when Federalist gentlemen not in favour of equality were in power. On the imposition of a new whiskey tax there was an insurrection around Pittsburgh, in the west of Pennsylvania, which was brutally quashed by the State militia.

On 1 March 1800, Colt arrived in Philadelphia to a very different reception. The recent election had brought the Democrats to power. Gentleman, Federalists like Colt, were not in power. He describes the anxious months in his *Narrative* as follows:

> A misunderstanding had arose in the minds of the Managers, by the instigation of Eneas [?] [Ennion] Williams, who had laid his plans to bring me into difficulty & dispute with the Company, he however failed in his designs – the result of the whole business was that after a minute investigation of my agency, my accounts was [sic] passed, my salary paid me during my continuance in the City, also my expenses for Board, Clerk hire, & requested still to continue in their employ – It was however an unpleasant controversy and the circumstances of being so long detained from my family was a matter which caused me much anxiety and on the whole the most unpleasant part of my life since arriving to State of Manhood.

The language is bitter. Arguably the bitterness, and the *Day Book* entries above, show that there was some truth in the allegations. Even if there had been no actual embezzlement, no 'creative accounting', Colt may have been more liberal than necessary with company funds; possibly, having an expense account for the first time had gone to his head a little. The incident certainly didn't endear him to his Colt relatives.

While he was being questioned by his managers in Philadelphia, Judah received two letters from his brother Samuel. Both letters ask the same question – is he able to confirm that he needs provisions from them for the following year? The first was sent in January: 'The only thing of importance to know is whether you engage in the service of the company for any longer time, whether any and what quantity of provisions will be wanted for the next season.'

He might well have been anxious. The *Day Book* reveals that in 1798 Samuel received $849 (worth around $17,000 in today's money) from the PPC for unspecified goods. Even allowing for Samuel Colt's original purchase price of the goods, this was a tidy sum – to gain, and to lose.

The second letter, dated Geneva, 18 March 1799, shrill in tone, starts:

Dear brother,

I received yours of the 19 Jan from Pittsburgh in which you engage that on your arrival at Philadelphia you would write me again and more fully. But whether from business, amusements of the city, ill health or what cause I know not, your promise has not been fulfilled. That you, who used scarcely to suffer one mail to pass without dropping me a line, should now spend two months at the Capital without even saying God Bless You, is a thing quite unprecedented ... Joseph and I have come to the conclusion of dissolving the partnership this Spring. We have already discontinued the store at Canandaigua and removed the goods here. I have taken a separate store and he takes the house for his family. I presume the measure will meet your approbation as the reason will be so obvious. ...

Geneva 18 March 1799,
#5945

Dear Brother

I received yours of the 19th Jany.
from Pittsburgh in which you engage that on
your arrival at Philadelphia you would write me
again and more fully. But whether from business
amusements of the city, ill health or what cause
I know not, your promise has not been fulfilled
    That you, who used scarcely to suffer one mail
to pass without dropping me a line, should now
spend two months at the Capital without even
saying God bless you, is a thing quite unprecedented. It is so unlike those examples of fraternal
affection heretofore given me, I am unwilling to
impute to so bold a cause as neglect, but will
think you are not in health or deeply engag'd
in business — However, far from being awed by
your silence I am about to write you a very lengthy
letter — Joseph & myself have come to the conclusion of dissolving partnership this spring. We
have already discontinued the store at Canl. and
removed the goods here. I have taken a seperate
store and he takes the house for his family. I
presume this measure will meet your approbation
as the reason will be so obvious. Although it was

Figures 31–33: Letter from Samuel to Judah Colt, 18 March 1799.[109]

[109] Sanford-Spencer Estate papers, Erie County Historical Society, Hagen Center, Erie.

Here is further proof of the complex interdependence between the extended Colt family and Judah's land agency.

Colt's enforced stay in Philadelphia finally came to an end in April 1801. His land agency was renewed, back dated. He was told to get back money that he had lent to Timothy Tuttle, but that seems to have been the only penalty; his managers may have felt that being forced to stay in Philadelphia for over a year was punishment enough. They had forced him to go over his accounts for 1797–9 in detail, and then had kept him waiting months for their verdict. His version of events remained that Williams had laid false claims against him which were proved unfounded.

*

Despite his victory at having his name cleared, Williams' accusation, minutely investigated by the PPC managers, had really shaken him. He arrived home at the end of May. It is interesting to read the account of his religious 'conversion' only three months later, on 27 September 1801. Mrs Colt was already a communicant – a convert to Presbyterianism. She encouraged Colt to accompany her to a Presbyterian open-air service 'in William Dundass's plantation, Greenfield.'

> ... while conversing with her I became more thoughtful than usual, and shortly after arriving at the place of meeting, I became more & more impressed with the evil nature of Sin, and of the importance of leading a sober, orderly & religious life, and it was not long after service began, that I found myself much disturbed in mind, & my body considerably agitated, and altho I felt a load of guilt upon me, I resolved to come forward and make a request to become a member of the Church... A token of admittance was given me by one of the Elders, I arose & took a seat at the Table. – So it was that Me and My beloved Consort were permitted both to partake of the Sacrament of the Lords Supper on the same day... (*Narrative*)

This service was part of a Feast – a familiar event at that period, when religious revival was sweeping through the United States. Tent meetings and conversions were commonplace; it seemed to go along with frontier life and indeed throughout the United States. There were also many 'missionaries' or travelling preachers, whom Colt records. He often accommodates them on their journeys. Robbins, historian of Erie County, explains that Presbyterianism was the favoured religion of the area – he puts it down to the New England influence.[110] The Colts will not have been the only family that night to be affected:

---

[110] Robbins, D.P. (1895), p. 167.

... now resolved that as for me & my house, we would serve the Lord and it became a duty to institute family worship, Morning and Evening, and to ask for a blessing to accompany the bounties of providence. (*Narrative*)

Here is an account of a chastened man. From this point, Colt begins to record business transactions meticulously in his *Journal*.

It is worth noting that the figures in his expenses are not out of line with those spent elsewhere out of Holland and Pennsylvania Population Company coffers. We know that Cazenove, when he first came to the United States, persuaded the Holland Land Company to part with $128,000 to set up Cazenovia (his own settlement in New York State) as a model community. He used the money to build, erect mills, give loans to store keepers. Despite all this, in 1800 the 'settlement' was abandoned – it had only attracted 27 settlers.[III] Ellicott, in his published accounts for 1798–1800, had expenses amounting to around $66,000. These huge annual outlays ensured that investing in land – especially for the Europeans who had put up the capital – was not and never would be the cash cow they had hoped for. Solid fortunes were made by the Colts and Ellicotts of the world.

The PPC managers had been particularly exercised at Colt's 'extending credit' to Colonel Timothy Tuttle, and Colt had been told to get this money back as soon as he could. Tuttle was a New Englander, a war hero and a gentleman. Tuttle proved a very important neighbour in disputes with the 'adverse settlers' and a loyal friend. But for the PPC managers briefed by Williams he had a poor credit rating, and was not to be trusted. Colt must have been pained to carry out this errand – which in the end was not easy to execute.

Held a long confab with Co T Tuttle respecting the money he owes the company, proposed returning the mills etc. for the debt

---

[III] Bingham, R.W. (1937), p. 41.

he owes them – he considers that building the mill was an advantage to the Company & that he ought to have indulgence – Spent some part of this day in the garden. (*Journal*, 22 June 1801)

*

Colt's life from this point settled into a regular pattern; when in Philadelphia on business he went to the theatre (*School for Scandal* by Sheridan on 4 February 1801), to the courts, wondered at the excesses he saw, dined with old friends from Connecticut or New York State; attended court on company business in Pittsburgh, with his lawyer Thomas Collins, who had become a friend. He followed the Federal cause in politics – he had been happy to report that he accompanied 65 settlers from Greenfield to Erie to vote in the election – all for the Federal candidate – on 10 October 1798.

He despised his opposite number, Joseph Ellicott, land agent of the Holland Land Company:

Thursday. Weather continuing pleasant for this season. Took an early set out and road about 40 miles, and put up at evening at a Mr Ross, behind Tontewandy Creek, where a Mr Joseph Eliott [Ellicott] is erecting a lot of mills, as is supposed for the Holland Co. Spent the evening with him at Mr Ross'. Mr. E. is a rank democrat. (*Journal*, 29 October 1801)

This incident is recorded more firmly still and with more detail, in his *Narrative*:

On the 26th of this month, October, I set out on a journey to Geneseo, State of New York, Enoch Marvin accompanyd me, at Batavia, on the waters of Tonewanta, we called on Joseph Ellicott, who was an acting agent for the Holland Land Company – Ellicott was a high toned Democrat, and not friendly disposed towards the emigrants from the Eastward from whence his principal Settlers come from.

On this same trip, according to the *Narrative* but not in the daily *Journal* – he sold the sloop *Washington* to a Mr Anstrul on Lake Ontario – only three years after it was built. He also decided to 'pay of a debt for a Tract of land, bought of Charles Williamson, situate on the Geneseo River it being a balance of $1390.50.' He is trying to tell his reader he was a man of business (selling a boat which is making a loss) and honour (paying his debts).

Colt spent time in his office reading each week – he mentions *The Life of Colonel James Gardiner, Who Was Slain at the Battle of Prestonpans, September 21, 1745*, by P. Doddridge (1747), and a five-volume *History of Europe* (1786) by William Russell, which was delivered to his address, volume by volume. He recorded in his *Journal* on Monday 8 February 1802, 'My evenings have been generally spent for several weeks past in reading Russel's History of Modern Europe, which is very well written and entertaining.'

He had a lively interest in farming methods. Here is the description of his visit to a famous Pennsylvania farmer to view his new techniques on 7 April 1803:

> Mr McAlister is perhaps the best practical farmer in Pennsylvania from whom I received much useful information, he also professes great mechanical talents... a large new barn, built on an improved construction. A large cyder house well constructed also a corn crib and Poultry house, Yards, Spring-House, House for Kiln drying tipple [hay]..Smoke House of wood superior to Stone or Brick, Horse Stable – He also has a Grist Mill, Salt mill, and Distillery well constructed as also a washing machien, the stream which supplies all his mills with water, also forms him a fish pond and waters all his meadows – he has between 40 & 50 acres of orchard of the best grafted fruits.

He mentions 'sundry kinds of Liquer made of Cherries' and that McAlister gave him 'a list of useful books to possess, viz Forsyth on Fruit Trees – Every Man his own Gardener by Thomas Main, The Botanic Garden printed by T.I. Snower, Agricultural Dictionary by N. Morton, printed 1799.'

All those books are English, from England. Thomas Mawe (not Main – Colt wrote that author down wrong) was gardener to the Duke of Leeds; 'The botanic Garden' seems to be a Cambridge University book published in 1796, and the *Agricultural Dictionary* was written by T. Morton (wrong initial), editor of the *British Agricultural Gazette*.[112] Political independence is one thing – the gaining of cultural independence quite another. Colt remained true to his British colonial origins even in his farming heroes.

As for Colt's personal life – he and his wife did finally have a child who survived beyond a few days – Eliza was born in July 1802 and survived long enough to be taken to Lyme to meet the Connecticut family. Sadly, Eliza died of a fever in 1805. This was at least the fourth child Mrs Colt had borne who died in infancy.

Colt's household, which had been five in 1800, and expanded again with the birth of Eliza, was joined by an Irish indentured lad in 1801, and a mulatto girl and her infant son in 1803. Colt tells us the mother had been reared in his father's house back in Connecticut. This woman, Chloe, was a chattel listed in Colt's father's will of 1788 when she was a little girl of five, bequeathed to Colt's mother. In 1802 Colt records asking to buy her from one Moses Sill, who must have acquired her, in Ontario County, New York State. Was she especially skilled at looking after young children, and therefore could she help with Eliza? They had already, on 20 March 1802, hired a girl to help: 'Thomas Hinton hired out daughter Hannah Hinton unto me this day for one whole year.' The Colt family had visited Lyme that winter, and began their return journey on 6 February 1803. Chloe was living with Judah's brother Joseph's family in Canandaigua at that time. On 17 March the same year there is an entry about a Chloe Bond in the *Journal*:

---

[112] Abercrombie, J. and Mawe, T. (1782), *Every Man His Own Gardener: Being a New, and Much More Complete Gardener's Kalendar Than Any One Hitherto Published*;Donn, J. (1796) *Hortus Cantabrigiensis: or, a Catalogue of Plants, Indigenous and Foreign, Cultivated in the Walkerian Botanic Garden,* Cambridge.

Timothy Tuttle, Thomas Robinson & John Phillips Esquire called on me and in their presence Chloe Bond bound herself to me for and until she becomes the age of 28 years – counting the time from the 6th of February last. The assessors of the poor bound her child Elijah to me also until he shall arrive to the age of 28 years.

Chloe's status as a slave may have ended, but it is almost unthinkable to 'bind' someone for as long as that – 13 years in her case and in Elijah's much longer.

Colt's *Journal* holds many entries about hospitality. Relatives come to stay, and friends – preachers, fellow land agents, lawyers. Thomas Collins, Timothy Tuttle, Major Alden, Thomas Rees, Jabez Colt, the last three all land agents. Another land agent who came to stay was a Dutch settler called Harm Jan Huidekoper. In1802 he records:

Sept 4. I set out again, and after a solitary ride of fifteen miles over a very bad road, where my horse fell once, I reached Greenfield, and was received with great cordiality by Mr Colt. This Mr Colt is a brother of my late fellow-traveller [he'd just left Jabez Colt], and, like him, is an agent of the Population Company of Pennsylvania.

The land along the road to Greenfield was fairly good, though here and there thin, and the clearings along part of the way seemed to me to have been made by New Englanders, being much better than those near Meadville. Mr Colt told me that my supposition was correct and that the settlers about here were in fact from New England. Greenfield itself has only six or seven houses and is insignificant. I stayed a day with the Colt family, treated with the utmost hospitality, which is natural to his race, and his kindness extended to accompanying me when I left, as far as the border of Pennsylvania, which is eleven miles from his house.[113]

[113] Tiffany, N.M. and F. (1904), *Harm Jan Huidekoper*, Cambridge: Riverside Press, p. 69.

Here is praise indeed. Although, knowing as we do that Greenfield and the country round was full of adverse settlers, the good husbandry he commended could as well have been the result of the Irish as of the Anglo-American New Englanders.

Colt, in his *Journal*, records very few items of national and international news. A rare example:

> From the newspapers and other channels of information were informed of Luisiana & New Orleans is seeded to the U. States – which by the ordinary course of events will add greatly to the wealth and respectability of the U. States.' (22 July 1803)

The words of a model citizen. Most items of international news go unmarked. Instead, he remained vexed with his 'intruders'. Every month or so there is another mention – here is a typical one from 20 June 1804:

> ... about half past 12 o'clock we returned home – [from Erie – he'd been to the Post Office] – on our way home & passing by a grass field opposite Joseph Shadducks we saw two men mowing & one other guarding them with a club. The conduct of Intruders is of all Rascals the most insulting.

The Colts move to Erie

In 1804 the Colts moved into a small house on one of his lots in Erie,

> by clearing of the Timber, repairing the house erecting a small Barn, which I afterward occupied a part of it for an office ... enclosed a piece of Ground for a Garden.... Close of this Year, 31st December 1804, found us quietly & happily situated in our new habitation in the Village of Erie.

Colt does not spell out why they moved. We can speculate that it might have been for the sake of the health of his wife and their frail baby daughter. Probably Greenfield had not continued to be the busy staging post the settlers had envisaged. This is how a later historian saw it:

In a short time Mr Colt saw his error and in 1804 he moved to Erie, where he remained the balance of his life.... On Mr Colt's departure, the greater portion of the colony [Greenfield] left also, scattering in various directions, and most of them making amends for their blunder by taking up some of the choicest lands in the County.[114]

Established in Erie, Colt continued with the PPC until it was dissolved in 1812, sold off at auction on behalf of the Company by Judah Colt and his brother Jabez Colt, the other PPC land agent in the Erie Triangle. The original shareholders barely got back their initial outlay.

The land companies never made the profits they had hoped:

It became apparent as the years went on that the company [the PPC] was never to realise the handsome profits visualised at the beginning. Heavy assessments were necessary to meet warranting and patenting fees and surveying expenses. Large amounts were expended to improve unsettled tracts in order to obtain patents on them. In 1797 and 1798 Judah Colt had from fifty to one hundred men busy, at company expense, improving tracts and resisting groups of intruders. Ennion Williams superintended twenty to thirty [company] men on Beaver Creek, in the south part of the Erie Triangle. Provisions and equipment were issued to settlers on credit, and these obligations remained on the books. Ejectment suits were numerous and costly. In several years, sales were not enough to provide the salaries of the agents. There is no evidence the company ever paid any dividends.[115]

Judah relied heavily on his two brothers-in-law, Elisha and Enoch Marvin, to keep the store in Greenfield and look after business in his annual absences in Philadelphia and New York on business. The other two Colt brothers remained in the Ontario County – storekeepers in Canandaigua, Almyra, and Geneva; there is an indication that Joseph set up business back in New

114 Bates, S.P. et al. (1884), p. 784.
115 Hale, R.N. (1949), p. 129.

York at some point because he is recorded as dying suddenly on a visit to his brother Samuel, then a well-established gentleman in Geneva, a generous donor to the academy, church warden.

In his latter years as a settled gentleman, Colt was burgess twice, in 1814–15 and 1822-4. He was an elder of the Presbyterian Church in Erie. He is mentioned in the histories of Erie as a trustee and benefactor of the academy, of the hospital, and a benefactor of the poor. In 1820, Colt built his last house, which survives (see Postscript). The three men richer than him in Erie in 1820 were (in order of wealth) Seth Reed from Massachusetts, Mr Kelso from Dauphin County, Pennsylvania and P.S.V. Hamot, a Frenchman.[116] He had by circumstance to get on with Europeans, and with Pennsylvanians – to learn to accept them into his circle. But in Erie County there were many well-to-do Connecticut families – many related by marriage – the Griswolds, the Marvins, the Seldens, and the Spencers. Judah Colt and Elizabeth Colt, like Judah Colt Spencer, remained New Englanders, settler colonists in the land west of the Alleghenies, to the end.

In 1818 Mrs Colt enters the public record. Before that she appears only in Colt's *Journal* – as his 'consort', his spiritual guide (never his housekeeper or overseer of the garden, the sewing, the cooking, and the dairy, though she must have done that throughout his marriage). With the wife of the other rich New Englander, Seth Reed, she set up a Sunday school.

In 1818, Mrs. Judah Colt, wife of the PPC land agent, collaborated with Mrs R.S. Reed and Mrs. Carr to establish a class of religious instruction on the Sabbath for girls, meeting alternately at the houses of the latter two ladies. Mrs Colt seemed to have been inspired by a visit back to her family home in New England, where schools of this type were common.[117]

[116] Bates et al. (1884), p. 513.

[117] Mary Cameron, M.E. (2001), 'The land developer's disputed frontier: A geographical interpretation of northwestern Pennsylvania settlement

And, to capture one of the other invisible groups, described as the 'Sunday School and Moral Society':

In May of 1821 the Erie Sunday School and Moral Society was organized, with original attendance of sixty-four, of all ages. In six months the attendance had increased to eighty-one, with a notation that twenty-one of those individuals were colored. As the 1820 census shows only thirty-four colored families (seventy-one individuals) in the county, they seemed to have captured a high proportion of the colored population in this organization.[118]

There may have been another explanation, if, as in the Connecticut style of Colt's childhood, the Native American, mulatto and black populations had all been swallowed up in this term 'coloured'.

After the demise of the PPC, Colt continued in the land business, and also in extending credit – in other words as a banker – from his Erie office. There are indications that he and Elizabeth took in at least three young relatives from back East, to finish their schooling and establish themselves. Another Judah Colt seems to have been the first. He inherited most of Colt's library – over 100 books.[119] The second was Thomas Colt, great grandson of Colt's grandfather, Benjamin Colt. Thomas was born and raised in Pittsfield, Massachusetts. He stayed in Erie and became a banker.

As Colt aged, he determined to make an heir to his business, and called, not on his brother's children or those of his brothers-in-law, who had moved west with him, but instead a great nephew, from Hadlyme in Connecticut, his older sister's grandson, Judah Colt Spencer. (This was my three times great grandfather, my grandmother's grandfather.) He does not record

1790–1820', dissertation, University of North Carolina: Chapel Hill, p. 181, quoting Bates's 1884 history of Erie County.

[118] Ibid.

[119] Journal of Judah Colt Spencer, 1834–5, transcript in author's possession.

why he brought this 16-year-old lad over to join his household in Erie in 1829, sent him to the Erie Academy, and set him to work in the office on land issues in his estate; we are left to surmise. The boy's mother, his niece, had married a military hero, William Spencer. This 'connection' by family might have consolidated Colt's reputation as a worthy first man of Erie and finally quashed any queries about his allegiances in '76. Or choosing him might have been a way of keeping the peace between his other, closer relatives. Or the name, so like his own, may have been reason enough. But this New England-bred lad was the main inheritor of Colt's business and lands.

Five years later, in 1832 Colt died, quickly, peacefully, of a stroke, leaving Judah Colt Spencer to pick up the reins of the business and look after his widow, Elizabeth, who in the event died two years later, leaving the young man in charge of many of the estates, church pews, land warrants, orchards, property and the business. He had farms and orchards in Canandaigua, in and around Greenfield (one of them on French Creek), and in Erie, some let out, some still worked. He asked his distant young cousin Thomas Colt to take on some of this work; what became of this young man is recorded below in the Postscript.

Colt's will[120] shows the extent of his estate – relatives were left parcels of land, settled and unsettled; they were left carriages, a library, farms, orchards, pews in the church. Judah Colt Esquire had done what he set out to do. He had become an Anglo-American gentleman. A true settler coloniser, he had obliterated all who had just claim to the lands he seized as his own – first the Native Americans, then the Irish. He did this by making them invisible, and where this wasn't possible, describing them as savages, drunks, fools, buffoons, using language to further disempower them. He used his 'entirely new country' to create anew the land of his youth, with all its social hierarchy and culture. He had done this with the help of fellow white settlers, and Federal and State laws. He had used his New England

---

[120] See Bibliography.

heritage as a weapon of respectability, to ensure that these were the values, the social norms, and this the architecture that dominated New York State and western Pennsylvania.

Colt had found a more awkward set of adversaries in the Erie Triangle – the Irish – who found their own champions in the Democrats – but eventually he used the power of the Land Companies, the local militia and the courts to gain the upper hand. All this was not done without some compromise, though he persisted in branding these other settlers as intruders, rascals well into the nineteenth century.

Colt had assured himself of the position he wanted, and the title of 'Esquire', not just by amassing capital but also through acquiring social standing.[121] All the late nineteenth-century histories of Erie County showed him to be a man 'of large estate'. His household in the Census of 1820 includes 11 people.

---

[121] In eighteenth-century and nineteenth-century Britain, and so also among New Englanders of the time, the term 'esquire' was applied to a commoner considered to have gained the social position of a gentleman.

Chapter 8

Conclusion

Colt's writings give us close-up information about two settlements, in two States, in the immediate aftermath of the Revolution. They give us a snapshot of a man, a social climber, making his way in the world of the 1780s and 1790s. His words confirm the story as historians currently tell it. Far from being a taming of the wilderness, a proud 'second creation', Colt's experience was that of a quick, brutal, overturn of a whole civilisation by colonists whose first thought was to recreate the landscape of their youth. Ontario County, New York and Erie County, Pennsylvania both prided themselves on being of New England. Both recreated the entire culture as closely as they could – the courts, the militia, the churches, the social hierarchies – above all the social hierarchies.

Colt demonstrates the huge power and influence of the New Englander in the history of the early frontier, and the ruthless use of networks to establish the primacy of his group, and above all to stamp social class on the new townships. Not that he and his kind were unopposed; his struggle with the poorer settlers demonstrates that the struggle for equality was alive and well. But the capital advantages rested with Colt and his kind, and Colt shows how these advantages could be exploited to the full.

The grammar school-educated, cultured Colt was able to use words to his advantage as well (despite some vagaries in spelling demonstrated in his *Journal*). Colt's words show the power of language in securing this victory – over Native Americans, over poor Irish, over the natural world. By not mentioning uncomfortable facts, such as Native Americans in the landscape;

by only mentioning set-piece quaint, needy Indians; by describing inconvenient Irish settlers as drunks and brawlers – he made himself and those like him seem by contrast normal and in control.

And his own story? He seized the opportunities offered him to make a fortune. He used his family connections, his friends, to secure his place. He had climbed the ladder and wanted to stay there. He marked his rise with the trappings of success at that time – houses with imported glass and cherry-wood floors; indentured servants. He became a church elder, a trustee of the turnpike.

Colt's story illustrates the settler colonial project of the Republic's early years – a project of conservative Anglo-American values, of rich white supremacy. It also demonstrates the complex routes seized by a conservative social climber of those years, richly illustrated by the words he uses, weapons in their own right.

Postscript

One final note – present day residents of Erie were recently offered the chance to live in Colt's last house, built in Erie in 1820. For many years it languished as a run-down multi-occupancy house, moved to Erie's poorer neighbourhood – but it has been recreated, as yet another appropriation, this time the present commodifying Colt's history – as he gained his fortune commodifying land; land that wasn't his in the first place.

Figure 34: Judah Colt's house in Erie, moved, dismantled, then moved again, reassembled and placed on the market.[122]

---

[122] The photograph was part of the advertisement.

Hon. Judah Colt House

Client: Erie Insurance and Thomas Hagen

Engineer – M.E.P: Kidder Wachter Jefferys Engineering

Contractor: Kidder Wachter Jefferys Construction

Summary: Deconstruction and Reconstruction of Historic House (circa 1820) with 2 apartments and new garage with additional 2 apartments

Hon. Judah Colt (1761–1832) one of Erie County's earliest citizens, settled at what is now known as Colt Station in 1796. As the agent for Pennsylvania Population Company, the county's first land developer, moved to the Borough of Erie in 1804. Colt served as Burgess of Erie in 1813 & 1820–1821. He built this Federal style house about 1820 at the South West corner of East 4th and French Streets where he entertained the Marquis De Lafayette (1757–1834) on June 3, 1825. This was also home to his nephew[123] Thomas G. Colt (1805–1861) the last Burgess and the first Mayor for the City of Erie. The house was moved in 1890 to 345 East Front Street and due to its poor condition was acquired, and dismantled in 2017. The building's existing conditions were drawn and each piece of lumber was labelled, dismantled and stored in a warehouse. In 2018, Judah Colt House and The Von Buseck House were rebuilt at their new location at the corner of 5th and German Streets in Erie, Pennsylvania. The Judah Colt House now has two 2-bedroom market-rate apartments with a new three-car garage behind it that has a two-bedroom apartment on the second floor.[124]

Apartment: $1,575 a month; includes landscaping and snow removal.

---

[123] Not his nephew, as explained above.

[124] Architect's advertisement: www.kidderwachter.com/projects/current/hon-judah-colt-house, downloaded 22 July 2020.

The author's relationship with the protagonist:
Seven generations, two hundred years

Deacon Joseph Colt = Desiree (Pratt) Colt

Deborah (Colt) Selden   **Judah (1761–1832)** = Elizabeth Marvin
| (no children survived infancy)
Deborah (Selden) Spencer
|
Judah Colt Spencer
|
William Spencer
|
Maud Dupuy (Spencer) Corbett
|
April (Corbett) Peretz
|
Elizabeth Peretz (1948–)

Deborah and Judah had six siblings: older brother Isaiah,
and Desiree, Assenath, Joseph, Samuel, and Jabez

Bibliography

Primary sources

Judah Colt: His Narrative, typewritten transcript, private collection of the author; also available (incomplete) from Cornell on line at https://babel.hathitrust.org/cgi/pt?id=coo.31924072102217&view=1up&seq=3, location of original unknown.

Judah Colt Journals 1796-1811, typewritten transcript, private collection of the author; also available from the Pennsylvania Historical Society, Philadelphia; location of original unknown.

Judah Colt, *Elements of Geometry: Laying of Land and Dividing Land*, March-April 1788, 40 pages, and *Geometrical Problems*, 22 January 1830, 64 pages, Sanford-Spencer Estate papers, Erie County Historical Society, Hagen Center, Erie. Box 20, ff4, unpublished.

Judah Colt, *Judah Colt Day Book 1798–9*, Erie County Historical Society, Hagen Center, Erie, manuscript.

Judah Colt, *Will*, https://www.ancestry.com/search/collections/8802/?name=Judah_Colt&e-Self-Civil1=1832_erie-erie-pennsylvania-usa_13849&name_x=s, downloaded 20 November 2020.

Judah Colt Spencer, *Journal 1834–5*, transcript in author's possession.

Pittsburgh Weekly Gazette, 10 June 1797, https://www.newspapers.com/search/#query=lands+for+Sale+or+Settlement&t=895&s_place=Pittsburgh%2C+PA&dr_year=1797-1797, downloaded 25 November 2020.

Sanford-Spencer Estate papers, Erie County Historical Society, Erie.

United States Census, 1790, Canandaigua, Ontario County, New York State.

United States Census, 1800, Greenfield, Erie County, Pennsylvania.

United States Census, 1820, Erie, Erie County, Pennsylvania.

Secondary sources

Abercrombie, J. and Mawe, T. (1782) *Every man his own gardener: Being a new, and much more complete gardener's kalendar than any one hitherto published*, London: Rivington.

Arbuckle, R. (1974) 'John Nicholson & the Pennsylvania Population Company', *Western Pennsylvania Historical Magazine* 57 (4), 353–5.

Bates, S.P. et al. (1884) *History of Erie County, Pennsylvania*, Chicago: Warner, Beers & Co., https://archive.org/details/cu31924096783489/page/n39/mode/2up, downloaded 24 November 2020.

Bayley, S. (2016) *The Private Life of the Diary: From Pepys to Tweets: A History of the Diary as an Art Form*, London: Random House.

Bingham, R.W. (ed.) (1937–41) *Reports of Joseph Ellicott as Chief of Survey (1797–1800) and as Agent (1800-1821) of the Holland Land Company's Purchase in Western New York*, Buffalo: Buffalo Historical Society Publications 32–33.

Blaakman, M. (2016) 'Speculation nation: Land and mania in the Revolutionary American Republic, 1776–1803', PhD thesis, Yale.

Blaakman, M. (forthcoming), *Speculation Nation: Land Mania in the Revolutionary American Republic*, Philadelphia: University of Pennsylvania Press.

Buck, S. and Buck, E. (1949) *The Planting of Civilization in Western Pennsylvania*, Pittsburgh: University of Pittsburgh Press.

Cameron, M.E. (2001) 'The land developer's disputed frontier: A geographical interpretation of northwestern Pennsylvania settlement, 1790–1820', dissertation, University of North Carolina, Chapel Hill.

Conzen, M.P. (ed.) (1994), *The Making of the American Landscape,* New York: Routledge (2nd edition).

de Crèvecoeur, J. Hector St John (1782) *Letters from an American Farmer,* London: Thomas Davies; reprint (1981), New York: Penguin.

Den Ouden, A.E. (2001) 'Against conquest: Land, culture, and power in the eighteenth-century histories of the native peoples of Connecticut', unpublished dissertation, University of Connecticut.

Donn, J. (1796) *Hortus Cantabrigiensis; or, a catalogue of plants, indigenous and foreign, cultivated in the Walkerian botanic garden, Cambridge*, Cambridge: Cambridge University Press.

Fenton, W. (1965) 'The journal of James Emlen Kept on a trip to Canandaigua, New York', *Ethnohistory* 12 (4) (Autumn), pp. 279–342, https://www.jstor.org/stable/480796, downloaded 23 March 2020.

Fischer, J.R. (1997). *A Well-executed Failure: The Sullivan Campaign against the Iroquois, July–September 1779,* Columbia: University of South Carolina Press.

Gallo, M. (2018), 'Improving independence: The struggle over land surveys in Northwestern Pennsylvania in 1794', *Pennsylvania Magazine of History and Biography* 142 (2), pp. 131–61, muse.jhu.edu/article/693339, downloaded 13 December 2020.

Gibson, R. (1798) *A Treatise of practical surveying; which is demonstrated from its first principles: Wherein everything that is useful and curious in that art, is fully considered & explained*, New York: William A. Davis & Co., 8th edition, www.surveyhistory.org/jacob%27s_staff1.htm, downloaded 19 May 2020.

Great Lakes Scuttlebutt (2016), 'Rare 18th century sloop Washington discovered in Lake Ontario', 24 August, https://www.greatlakesscuttlebutt.com/news/press-room/rare-18th-century-sloop-washington-discovered-in-lake-ontario/, downloaded 11 December 2020.

Hale, R.N. (1949) 'The Pennsylvania Population Company', *Pennsylvania History*, 16 (2), pp. 122–30.

Heinmiller, G.L. (2010) *Craft Masonry in Ontario, Seneca and Yates Counties, New York,* Onondaga and Oswego Masonic District Historical Society, https://nanopdf.com/download/craft-masonry-in-ontario-seneca-yates_pdf, downloaded 24 November 2020.

Hurd, D.H. (1882) *History of New London County, Connecticut, with Biographical Sketches of Many of Its Pioneers and Prominent Men*, Philadelphia: J.B. Lippincott & Co., http://dunhamwilcox.net/town_hist/nl-chap12.htm, downloaded 3 April 2018.

Linklater, A. (2015) *Owning the Earth: The Transforming History of Land Ownership*, London: Bloomsbury.

Mancini, J.R. (2009) 'Beyond reservation: Indian survivance in southern New England and eastern Long Island, 1713–1861', PhD thesis, University of Connecticut.

Mancini, J.R. (2015) 'In contempt and oblivion: Censuses, ethno geography, and hidden Indian histories in eighteenth-century southern New England', Mashantucket Pequot Museum and Research Center, *Ethnohistory*, 62 (1), pp. 61–94.

McIntosh, W.H., Hanger, G.M., Pitts, C.P. (1876) *History of Ontario Co., New York: with illustrations descriptive of its scenery, palatial residences, public buildings, fine blocks, and important* manufactories, Philadelphia: Everts, Ensign & Everts.

Middlekauff, R. (1961) 'A persistent tradition: The classical curriculum in eighteenth-century New England', *William and Mary Quarterly* 18 (1), pp. 54–67.

Morgan, L.H. (1851) *The League of the Ho-dé-no-sau-nee or Iroquois*, Rochester, New York.

Nye, D. (2003) *America as Second Creation: Technology and*

Narratives of New Beginnings, Cambridge: MIT Press.

Oberg, M.L (2016) *Peacemakers: The Iroquois, the United States, and the Treaty of Canandaigua, 1794*, Oxford: OUP.

O'Reilly, H. (1838) *Sketches of Rochester*, Buffalo: William Alling, https://archive.org/details/sketchesofroches00orei, downloaded 20 July 2020.

Porter, A. (1904) *Narrative of Early Years in the Life of Judge Augustus Porter,* Buffalo: Buffalo Historical Society Publications 7, pp. 277–330.

Potter, C.E. (1888) *Genealogies of the Potter Family and Their Descendants in America,* Boston: Alfred Mudge and Son.

Rittner, D. (1999) *Lansingburgh*, New York: Arcadia Publishing.

Robbins, D.P. (1895) *Popular History of Erie County, Pennsylvania*, Erie: Advertiser Printing Co.

Russell, W. (1779) *The history of modern Europe. With an account of the decline and fall of the Roman Empire, and a view of the progress of society, from the fifth to the eighteenth century. In a series of letters from a nobleman to his son.* London: Robinson, Robinson, Walter and Sewell.

Sanford, L.G. (1861), *The History of Erie County, Pennsylvania*, Philadelphia: J.B. Lippincott & Co., enlarged and privately reprinted, 1894.

Silveus, M. (1935) 'McNair correspondence: Land problems in Northwestern Pennsylvania', *Western Pennsylvania Historical Magazine* 18, pp. 237–54.

Simmons, B. (1997) 'A window opens to Erie's Past: "Judah Colt Daybook, Greenfield, 1798–1799"', *Journal of Erie Studies* 26 (1), pp. 5–23; also available at: https://sites.rootsweb.com/~paerie/townships/Greenfield/JudahColtArticle.html, downloaded 4 July 2020.

Simmons, B. (2002) *Rees' Pieces*, Harborcreek Historical Society, https://sites.rootsweb.com/~paerie/famhist/ReesVPart1.htm, downloaded 10 July 2020.

Simmons, B. (2016) *The Lowry Clan*, Erie County (PA) Genealogy, Family Histories, https://sites.rootsweb.com/

~paerie/famhist/LowryClan2P1.htm, downloaded 24 November 2020.

Soodalter, R. (n.d.) 'Massacre and retribution: The 1779-80 Sullivan Expedition', on Historynet, https://www.historynet.com/massacre-retribution-the-1779-80-sullivan-expedition.htm, downloaded 13 December 2020

Spencer, H.R. (1962) *Erie: A History*, private publication, in this author's possession.

Taylor, A. (1996) *William Cooper's Town: Power and Persuasion on the Frontier of the Early American Republic*, New York: Vintage.

Taylor, A. (2001) *American Colonies: The Settling of North America*, New York: Viking Penguin.

Taylor, A. (2006) *The Divided Ground: Indians, Settlers, and the Northern Borderland of the American Revolution*. New York: Knopf.

Taylor, A. (2016) *American Revolutions: A Continental History, 1750–1804*, New York: Norton.

Tiffany, N.M. and F. (1904), *Harm Jan Huidekoper*, Cambridge: Riverside Press, https://babel.hathitrust.org/cgi/pt/search?q1=%244%2C000+&id=uc2.ark%3A%2F13960%2Ft3rvoh18k&view=1up&seq=95&num=69, downloaded 14 December 2020.

Turner, F.J. (1921) *The Frontier in American History*, New York: H. Holt and Co., http://www.gutenberg.org/files/22994/22994-h/22994-h.htm, downloaded 6 July 2020.

Turner, O. (1850) *Pioneer History of the Holland Purchase of Western New York*, Buffalo, New York: Buffalo : Geo. H. Derby and Co., https://books.google.co.uk/books/about/Pioneer_History_of_the_Holland_Purchase.html?id=N976piQog8kC&printsec=frontcover&source=kp_read_button&redir_esc=y#v=onepage&q&f=false, downloaded 6 July 2020.

Turner, O. (1851) *History of the Pioneer Settlement of Phelps and Gorham's Purchase, and Morris' Reserve*, Rochester, New York:

William Alling, https://play.google.com/store/books/
details?id=VlIWAAAAYAAJ&rdid=book-VlIWAAAAYAAJ&
rdot=1, downloaded 11 July 2020.

Winchester, S. (2013), *The Men Who United the States*, London:
William Collins.

Lightning Source UK Ltd.
Milton Keynes UK
UKHW021356290321
381184UK00011B/3104